THE CORE

Exercising Godly Character through the
Nourishment of Spiritual Fruit

THE CORE

*Exercising Godly Character through the
Nourishment of Spiritual Fruit*

DR. CANDUS JACK-WILLIAMS

Library of Congress Control Number: 2019908992
ISBN: Hardcover   978-1-7960-4448-5
               Softcover   978-1-7960-4447-8
               eBook   978-1-7960-4446-1

Print information available on the last page.

Rev. date: 07/31/2019

To order additional copies of this book, contact:
Xlibris
1-888-795-4274
www.Xlibris.com
Orders@Xlibris.com
799333

CONTENTS

ACKNOWLEDGEMENTS

Through the mighty and divine strength from God, this book was established. I thank God for allowing me to be obedient in this journey as well as allowing me to reflect on His love. I would like to thank those who have challenged me to persevere through hardships and those who encouraged me to keep my dream alive.

I thank my father, Wilson Jack, Jr., who has always encouraged me no matter what. Although he is not here in the physical form, I thank God for allowing me to have such a present father and faithful male figure. I thank my mother, Barbara Jack for esteeming me and supporting me in my endeavors.

Thank you to my loving sister and best friend, Tonya Thomas, who has been such a huge support in this process. I thank you for supporting me with my vision and ideas along with honest feedback. Thank you Cori Thomas for sharing her with me as I endured trying times. Through ups and downs, you both have been there with consistency. Thank you for being patient with me. You are significantly valued. Thanks to Rebecca Rodgers, sister, for believing in me and supporting me in so many ways. I thank my brother, John Jack, for being a protector and fulfilling a father-like role in our lives.

I thank my son, Treylan Brown who is such an inspiration to me. Your presence is a constant reminder of the fact that God is near us and that He hears our prayers. You are such a beautiful child and I am so captivated by the joy and peace that is within you.

I thank my husband, Alex Williams, Sr., for encouraging me with this vision.

To such a wonderful friend, Antoinette Jenkins and her family, you have been so supportive of me. Words can't express how much your kindness inspires me.

To Corry Williams, little did you know that you prompted me to write about the fruit of the spirit. I thank you for trusting me to lead devotions, for your knowledge of the word of God, your discipline and self-control, and for your enthusiastic energy that radiates among many.

To Dr. John R. Adolph, Pastor at Antioch Missionary Baptist Church in Beaumont, TX, more than you know your messages have been so impactful. Your gentle spirit is also infectious. Keep allowing God to use you, as you are still a blessing to so many in various ways.

To Dr. Remus Wright, Pastor and Co-Pastor Mia K. Wright at the Fountain of Praise in Houston, TX, you have been such an inspiration to me. Your obedience, drive, and commitment to saving souls is remarkable. You both are great examples of what goodness is. I commend you both.

INTRODUCTION

Have you ever looked forward to something for such a very long time with expectancy, hope, and desire, but realized God had a completely different plan for you? Have you ever faced hardships, and just when you thought you were making a breakthrough, more issues came knocking at your door? Have you faced a tough challenge and did your best to endure it all to realize the problem did not only linger, it grew larger than before?

Like many of you, this happened to me. I was battling an issue that was beyond my control. In fact, it was beyond what I foresaw I could possibly encounter. As confident as I was, and as God-fearing as I thought I was, I was not prepared for what I was about to experience.

In many cases, we find ourselves fighting battles we would never elect to fight. To my testament, I journeyed through a situation that was so inimitable it had to be God-led. No matter how careful we are in life, we can never escape God's plan. We may prolong the journey, but His will shall be done. At the height of my problems, I connected to God on a deeper level and later learned to value Him much more. Because of the type of situation I encountered, I felt God was tugging for my attention. In hindsight, I can truly say I am grateful. At the height of my problems; however, I was in sudden shock, confusion and pain.

UNEXPECTED TRIALS

So what happens when life takes you on a journey you are not prepared for? What happens when your back is pressed against the wall and it seems there is no way to maneuver out? What happens when you have been in a battle with the enemy and you felt like you have been knocked out, even if you feel you did not deserve it? How do you get back up? When do you get back up? Some would even ask, "Why even try to get back up?" No one said that life would be easy. Each of us has a unique journey ahead of us. Why? Because God has a special plan for our lives. Everything about him is extraordinary. So when we find ourselves experiencing situations that appear to be too peculiar for us to understand, it's probably because God is trying to tell us something and He's trying to prevent us from getting too caught up in our situations to hear Him.

Sometimes we are hit so hard that we forget how to get back up. When soaked in pain, despair, and devastation, it is easy to make unsound decisions and not rationalize each move we make, especially when we are deep in our emotions. Think about how a boxer reacts to a knockout. Once they have been impacted by the hit, they do not immediately get back up because they have not regained consciousness. If they get back up prematurely, they may stagger in an unprepared stance to fight against their opponent. However, if they lay helpless too long, their 10-second count will expire.

Life is about knowing what moves to make and when to make them. We may encounter some moments when we'll stagger or even get knocked down, but we must make a decision thereafter. Knowing that we may not win every battle makes it easier to accept the fact that we are not supposed to because the battle is not our own. God will always win the war *if we just allow Him to help us during our fight.*

Establishing a relationship with God helps us develop what I call a crazy faith. This relationship is so special because in it, God will give us the handbook we need to maneuver through life directly through Him. If you want peace, understanding, joy, restoration, strength, wisdom, protection, you name it, He will provide them all willingly. In this relationship, God will become acknowledged within in our foundation, our core. All we need to do is exercise God's power within us! Like a seed, if we do not water it and provide it with sunlight after we plant it, it will not grow. My goal is to help you learn how to nurture your relationship with God through daily exercises to produce God-like character and help you grow spiritually.

THE CORE

Every living thing has a core. Every structure has some sort of foundation. The core of the human body consists of all muscles in the midsection that work to stabilize the entire body. Many athletes use their core to support faster and longer throws, harder batting or boxing swings, and quicker movement for running. However, strength and endurance is built on exercise. Know that the enemy is also competing and without consistent practice from our end, our opponent will outperform us. It is merely up to us to exercise our core so that we are able to stand on solid ground.

The enemy is constantly battling God's anointed; therefore, it is important we take up the full armor of God (Ephesians 6:10-18) to fight against their attacks. The bible is filled with scriptures warning us that the stronger our relationships with God get, the harder the devil will attack. Just as a house made of sticks, without a strong core or foundation, we will crumble each time a storm hit us. Each chapter in this book provides ways to acquire God-like character, which is the fruit of the spirit, to help us strengthen our walk with God holistically (mind, body, and spirit), hence building a strong core through daily exercise. I pray that this book will help you build your faith and strengthen your walk with God the same way writing this book has for me, no matter what challenges you may encounter.

CHAPTER 1

EXERCISING YOUR MIND

Have you ever really wanted something in life you just could not get your mind off of? Perhaps it's a new home, starting a business, or growing a family. Maybe it's a career change or simply finding Mr. or Mrs. Right. Many of you may have learned that anything we want in life do not come without a cost. Whether it's our labor, our time, or money, we typically make investments towards what we want to accomplish.

Since I was a little girl, I was always intrinsically motivated to be successful. It was at a point where I often competed with myself. I always remembered being "in my head," and constantly thinking about how I could do things better.

I am the third child out of four children, so maybe it was my way of standing out. Regardless, I contribute a lot of my work ethic to my parents who had high expectations for us. I grew up in a rural area in a nice home amongst working parents who had big dreams for us. They worked hard to ensure we had all the essentials. We found out later in life that the biggest essential they strived to provide us with was a healthy relationship with God.

As children, we felt like we lived in the church. Both of our parents sang in the choir, and my mother helped clean the church on weekends while my father mowed the church lawn. We also spent the majority of our Sunday mornings and afternoons in Sunday school and church service. Although as a child, I did not understand how to establish a relationship with God nor understood how to pray to Him, I was exposed to many testimonies and knew that God was real and important.

Because of my upbringing and structured household environment, I was often influenced to work hard. In addition, I had family support and encouragement to help me through tough times. Although I grew up in an ideal family household, it does not mean I did not face challenges. I faced many and still face them today. However, it's not about what challenges nor how many challenges we face, it's how we live through them that helps us live abundantly.

POWER OF THE MIND

Suppose you are faced with a job loss and suddenly you find yourself evicted from your apartment or foreclosed on the home you owned. Now you are homeless and forced to live with a friend or even in your car. You have a choice to either get a new job so that you can save money to acquire the things you once had or commit to robbery or a related crime. It's actually scary when you do not know how long you will remain in this process, especially when working hard and can barely make ends meet. One thing that we must understand is that our minds are very powerful. We can deposit good thoughts into it or bad thoughts. God is one voice that fills our heads with wisdom, peace, understanding, protection, love, strength, discernment and so much more. However, if we disconnect from Him, we will not retain much.

The other voice we may hear is the voice of Satan. He is constantly nagging at us, filling our heads up with lies. He tells us that we should give up, that no one will hire us, and we will never get through tough circumstances. He will really nag us in our periods of wait by encouraging us to think that God has left us and that He does not love us. We must understand that we have a choice to decide on which voice we will give power to. The voice of God, or Satan.

If we fill our minds with positive thoughts, we will fall back on those thoughts when we hit a bump along the road. Will life be perfect? Never. But those positive thoughts will fuel us with motivation and hope to persevere through rough moments. If we listen to Satan's lies, then we result to doubt, fear, insecurities, inadequacies, thus, leading to us making knee-jerk decisions that could cause more damage than we currently face.

Satan has a way of diminishing our faith in God through our minds. 2 Corinthians 10:4 states, "For the weapons of our warfare are not of the flesh, but have divine power to destroy strongholds" (ESV). Our mind is our stronghold. There is so much power in the way we think. When Satan encourages us to relinquish faith in God, we allow him to become our stronghold and destroy our power. Environmental, cultural and social influences could affect how we think; however, they are not excuses for our lack of personal connections with God.

Despite of what challenges we face, we can still walk with grace and be encouraging to others in our times of need. If we all learn to strengthen our minds, we will then show in our actions that we are more than conquerors.

FUNCTIONS OF OUR MINDS

So how do our minds work? First, we must understand that there are three main functions of our minds. They are thinking, feeling, and wanting. If we think about it, we exercise these functions each day continuously. We are constantly thinking about what to do, when to do it and how to do it. We also feel the way we think at times, and we want what is on our minds based on how we feel. Our minds are very powerful because the way we think can determine how we may feel throughout the day.

Have you ever heard of the expression, "I woke up on the wrong side of the bed?" This indicates that I'm not feeling my best and that I could ultimately not have a good day. Maybe you did not get enough sleep the night before, or you did not get a chance to grab coffee before work.

Perhaps, you went to bed worried and stressed, only to wake up the same way. The function of thinking consists of making sense of things that occurred in our lives. It tells us what is happening around us to help us figure things out. As thinkers, we judge, analyze, compare, perceive, determine, and synthesize what is going on in our lives constantly. If we think that we cannot function without our morning coffee, we will feel that way, thus, carry a negative outlook for what is to be expected in our day simply based on the fact that we lacked something.

The second function of our minds is feeling. This has a direct relationship of what we think at a particular point in our day. This function evaluates how positive and negative things are in our lives and tells us how we should feel about some of the things we experience. It is not easy to not think about the problems we face and situations that occur beyond our control, especially if we are still working through them. If we think about the last example I gave about losing a job, many of us know that finding a good job is not always going to be a fast and easy process. Because of worry and stress about paying bills, after many unsuccessful attempts in the job search, many people would feel stressed and too fatigued to move forward. When we "get in our feelings", we often make decisions based on how we are feeling. Unfortunately, because of that, we make decisions that could lead to unwanted consequences.

This leads me to the last function of the mind. The last function is wanting. When we want something, we typically act on it. This function stirs purpose, motives, goals, desires and values. When we want something, we usually pursue it with energy. But what happens when we put on all of this great positive energy into something to receive rejections? How can we strengthen our minds when we are not only exercising a want, but a need?

Trust me when I tell say that I know what it is like to need to find work while bills are piling up or what it is like to take care of someone while feeling tired. I even know what it's like to pull it together on the outside when things inside of the home are falling apart. There are basic needs in life that can cause stress when trying to fulfill them. We all have an innate desire to succeed, so when we do not reach that point it is disappointing. Ephesians 4:23 encourages us to be renewed in the spirit of our minds. Although external factors can stir up unexpected emotions, joy and peace formulate from our thoughts through God's divine presence.

Thoughts reveal what we expect in our circumstances. Many things that we experience in life are beyond our control because God wants to teach us two things. The first thing is that our battles do not belong to us; they belong to the Lord (2 Chronicles 20:15). We as Christians are always trying to handle things on our own. God allows trauma or tragic experiences to occur just to show us how powerful He is. We must understand that God can transform things if we just allow Him to. In the process, we must totally surrender our hearts, minds, and spirits to function properly when life throws curve balls at us.

We go to God in prayer asking Him why and how, but instead of waiting for a response from Him, we end our prayers only to discover that we asked God for advice without the intention of really seeking it; yet we never took the time to wait for His response. Throughout this book, I will provide you with information that will help you develop your prayer life and build personal relationships with God.

THE ENEMY

Although we go to battle against the enemy daily, it is important to also understand that the enemy plays mind games with us. Think about someone who has deceived you before- perhaps an ex-boyfriend or girlfriend. During the dating stage of your relationship, they may have played tricks with your mind to perceive that they would treat you right because they studied who you were. Even thieves study their next victim's patterns and many criminals know the court system better than some attorneys do. When we become edified in the word of God, we form wisdom, which helps us reach a place of discernment.

The Bible indicates that Satan was one of God's angels. He knows and understands scriptures better than some evangelists understand them. He knows even better than many Christians how powerful God is based on what he has witnessed from God. He desires God's authority because of his *knowledge* of who God is. "…Satan himself masquerades as an angel of light" (2 Corinthians 11:14, NIV). He is a deceiver, and knowing that, we should be prepared to not fall into the traps created by Satan.

The devil often puts on a disguise to make it look like he stands for good, but he is actually leading people towards failure the entire time. Pedophiles may lure children by befriending them or with treats all with a motive to fulfil their selfish desires. In Matthew 4:1-11, the devil made an offer to feed Jesus by turning rocks into bread. However, Jesus was wise to realize that Satan was trying to deceive Him. He stated that Satan, "…was a murderer from the beginning, not holding to the truth, for there is no truth in him. When he lies, he speaks his native language, for he is a liar and the father of lies" (John 8:44, NIV).

Many times we say that the devil is in our way, but aside from the enemy, we are in our own way. We claim we love God, but do not know God's word the way we should, have not spent time with Him like we need to, nor trusted Him the way should. We can't go into a classroom and expect to pass a test because we simply like the instructor or say that we trust that the instructor is good at his or her job. It is up to us to pay attention to instructions and study the content so that we can apply what we know, especially when we really need to. 1 John 4:4, states, "Greater is He that is in you, than he that is in the world" (KJV). The enemy knows that God's power lies dormant in our spirit. We just have not activated it! Once we trigger it, we must exercise it. Our journey towards victory begins based on how we think. If only we knew how great God is to us and for us, then we can shift our thinking to another level.

The second thing is that God wants to know if we truly trust Him. Our faith in Him is constantly being tested. God ordained a path for us to walk on, but it is up to us to decide whether we will follow His path and this is simply based on how our minds operate. We speak with our lips that we love God and trust in Him, but when things do not occur the way we want them to, we often allow our flesh to take priority over our spirit.

Trust me, it is not easy because we do what naturally feels right to our flesh. If we are hungry, we eat. If we are tired, we rest. If we are thirsty, we drink. So it is easy to panic when things happen in our lives that are unsettling because of discomfort and fear. If we truly expect something to happen in our lives, ordained by the will of God, we should not fear that it will not occur.

Daniel and the Lion's Den

We can not allow our thoughts and emotions to betray us and rob us of our peace and victory. We must set an expectation to win. Ephesians 4:24 states that we should "put on a new self, created to be like God in true righteousness and holiness" (NIV). This scripture reminds me of the story of Daniel in the lion's den.

God used Daniel to save a nation because Daniel refused to bow to man. Daniel, leader of advisors was a faithful believer and follower of God. His love for God was well known. He too had enemies. Some of us call them haters- not because Daniel did anything to them, but because they saw something special in Daniel and that he was favored. Instead of loving him, they became jealous of him, which is a dangerous emotion to have. Other men despised him so much that they devised a plan to get rid of Daniel. They told King Darius, ruler over Babylon to create a law to forbid people from worshipping other Gods. If they broke the law, they would be thrown into the lion's den to be eaten and destroyed.

Daniel was aware of this law; however, he was committed to serving God. His mind and flesh could have told him to take heed to the new law, but his faith and love for God in his heart allowed him to not only remain steadfast in his prayer, but also in his praise! Let me pause here and say that when we feel we are being attacked or even viewed as an underdog amongst people around us, it's easy to retreat. Daniel had an expectation to win and he knew that he could only find victory in God alone, not by his own might, and definitely not by control of man. Daniel prayed several times daily, even in the view of others, but all with good intentions of pleasing God. When the men who plotted against him saw this, they told King Darius, who favored Daniel. Heartbroken, King Darius honored the law and sent Daniel into the lion's den, where he was trapped behind a stone.

Put yourself in the shoes of Daniel at this very moment. Daniel could have easily felt that the enemy got his way. I'm quite sure he was terrified as he entered into the lion's den. Wouldn't you? However, his actions leading up to that point showed how committed he was to serving God. Daniel's faith in God was tested the entire time!

The next day, King Darius went over to check on Daniel, surprised to find out that Daniel was alive and woundless. Daniel stated to the king in Daniel 6:21, "My God sent His angel, and He shut the mouths of the lions. They have not hurt me because I was found innocent in His sight" (NIV). We too can be an example of what God can do for us with a surrendered heart, like Daniel. He did not surrender to the enemy, but to God alone. The enemy wants us to surrender to him. He wants us to give up because he sees God's mighty power within us.

It first starts with a shift in how we think. Not only was Daniel's life spared, but also God received glory from the king and the nation and Daniel prospered during the reign of Darrius. What a win-win situation! By living in God's presence, we can allow the Holy Spirit to renew our thoughts and attitudes. Throughout this book, I will share with you how to live in God's presence and how that could help you transform. God should be at the core of everything we do each day. Through sowing and pruning, will we reap the harvest of His spiritual fruit.

CHAPTER 2

EXERCISING YOUR CORE: GOD'S SPIRITUAL FRUIT

The definition of core is the central and most essential part of anything (*Cambridge English Dictionary*, 2019). Genesis 1:26-29 states that we are created in the image of God, in His likeness and under His authority. Because we are made through the spirit, it is vital that we take care of it, being that the spirit is the core of our existence. Adam became a living being when God breathed the breath of life into him (Genesis 2:7). Because the spirit is the core of humans, it is the Holy Spirit that gives us real life.

When compared to fruit, think of the core as the fleshiest part of it. Some fruit contain seeds in the flesh that we consume while others fruit do not. Fruit has different character, but are beneficial and produce seeds. The seeds of fruit are units of reproduction that serve several functions for plants that produce them. Without the seeds, it is impossible to produce fruit, and when fruit is not produced, there is no harvest. Thus, it is essential for us to nurture our seeds (spirit) so that we can grow and develop a holy life and Jesus-like character.

There are several elements of the Holy Spirit. They are defined as spiritual fruit. Galatians 5:22-23 states, "But the fruit of the Spirit is love, joy, peace, patience, kindness, goodness, faithfulness, gentleness, self-control…" (ESV). The fruit of the spirit is God's love and work within us that flows through the Holy Spirit. God allows us the ability to reflect His character through His fruit, and the better our relationship is with God, the easier and more effective we can access His fruit.

Think about the relationship a personal trainer has with a client. They first provide the trainee with information about their health. They eventually provide them with a diet and exercise plan, then monitor their progress over a period of time after the trainee became committed to the program. God is our personal trainer whom gives us direction on what love and faith looks like, how to find peace and joy, when to be patient, why self-control is important, and how to display kindness, goodness, and gentleness even when we are in a tough season.

Like a diet, if we do not abide by the expectations the trainer set for us, nor stay committed to the program, we will not see the results we desire. We may notice that often, the trainer push us to exceed our goals because they have faith that beyond their time spent with us in training, we will independently live a healthier lifestyle. God is the same way. He has these spiritual gifts that He cannot wait to give us. If we want them bad enough, we must put in more effort to obtain them.

These gifts are not free, but God wants us to access and delight in them. Each day, God blesses us with life! What a blessing! God continues to bless us with health and strength, functioning minds, food, and even while we are sleeping God protects us from attacks that can occur during the night. Even during times we disobeyed and made poor decisions, God provided us with mercy along with gracing us during difficult moments. Those are just some of the gifts God gives us daily, free of charge because he loves us so much. Don't get me wrong, the stronger our relationship is with God, the more gifts He will provide; however, if there is ever a moment when we decide to take a break from praying or when we stray from God, He will still provide, but it is important to never take His mercy for granted.

Many parents who love their children may want to provide them with more than they had growing up in relation to clothing, better schools, morals, social experiences, and love. We know that our children may disappoint us at times, but we love them so much unconditionally, (and with a little tough love added) that no matter what, we will show them mercy, then teach them to be better. That is how God is with us. Even when we do not show gratitude, he still supplies us with essentials.

God wants to provide us with His spiritual gifts, but we must work for it. Spiritual fruit is God's *love* and *work* in us that flows through the Holy Spirit in and out. As I stated before, God wants us to access them- so He is willing to provide us with it. He is simply telling us that we must work for it. His fruit is so precious that it can not be acquired easily. If we want something, such as more money, we know that we have to get out and work for it. The more we want, the harder we have to work for it. We must want it bad enough! Unfortunately, many people do not strive to obtain them for these reasons: either they do not know how good it is for us and to us, or they do not want to put in the work to fight the flesh. Galatians 5:17-23 states:

> For the flesh lusts against the Spirit, and the Spirit against the flesh; and these are contrary to one another, so that you do not do the things that you wish. But if you are led by the Spirit, you are not under the law. Now the works of the flesh are evident, which are: adultery, fornication, uncleanness, lewdness, idolatry, sorcery, hatred, contentions, jealousies, outbursts of wrath, selfish ambitions, dissensions, heresies, envy, murders, drunkenness, revelries, and the like; of which I tell you beforehand, just as I also told you in time past, that those who practice such things will not inherit the kingdom of God (NKJV).

God's spiritual fruit will develop your character. Man's definitions of the spiritual fruit is misleading when compared to God's vision. If God created us to be like Him, we must know and understand that love, joy, peace, patience, kindness, goodness, faithfulness, gentleness, and self-control are not character traits that will be easy to exercise.

The spirit is constantly fighting against the flesh, which means anytime we resist something, it takes work. With that being said, obtaining spiritual fruit is deeper than simply saying we have joy today or that our faith is strong. Believe it or not, we do it often. I can say that I own designer clothing and that I drive an expensive car, but that does not make me rich either. I can have a yard filled with various fruit trees, but if I do not eat the fruit and delight in them consistently, the nutrients within the fruit will not help my body thrive.

The Apostle Paul said that fruitfulness is tied to the knowledge of God (Colossians 1). Our flesh tells us it's natural to love only those who love us back, but the spirit tells us to love our enemies. The flesh makes us feel that we only find joy during happy times, but the spirit shows we can find joy during difficult times. The flesh demonstrates that when our troubles go away we will have peace, but it was stated in Hebrews (13:5), "I will never leave you nor forsake you" (ESV); therefore, we can experience peace in our times of struggle. The flesh tells us that we cannot wait long before we receive whatever we desire, but the spirit says that longsuffering will occur and that patience builds character. The flesh wants us to be kind and good and gentle to those who show favor towards us, but the spirit says we should be kind, good and gentle to those who don't as well, because they may need it the most. The flesh wants us to make sense of everything, and see things before they happen, yet the bible says to "…walk by faith, not by sight" (2 Corinthians 5:7) (NKJV). And we know the flesh wants us to react when tempted, but the spirit wants us to show good temperament and have self-control.

In order to bear good fruit, we must abide in the Lord. He is our safe house. What we produce as sowers is consistent with our experiences with God. If God is in us, then what comes out of us should be God-like character. Various fruit, such as apples, oranges, peaches, strawberries, pineapples, coconut, etc… contain different nutrients that will naturally keep the human body in a healthy condition. Because they are each composed of different nutrients, and because the body needs a variety of nutrients to function, we cannot just live off one fruit.

We need elements from each to survive. We cannot get into the Kingdom by bearing only one fruit. We must embody them all. In other words, being kind will not get you into heaven alone.

Character must be developed and that occurs with a little resistance from the flesh. I remember a time when I wanted something new to occur in my life. Because it was not happening, I asked God for patience. I felt like He was forcing me to be patient, so I thought that by asking for it would help me get through that season of wait. Little did I know what I was asking for! I asked for patience and God gave me a plate of tests with a side of trials. Trust me when I say that they were not easy. Each one became even more difficult, not because I got into any trouble, but because I did not exercise patience the way He wanted me to.

God was trying to plant something within me, but I did not let it settle. My period of wait became so uncomfortable that I focused on the desire and grabbed on to worries, burdens, and fears. My way of enduring the wait was all wrong. So God decided to make several attempts to teach me until I could get it right.

We generally feel that when we are enduring periods of wait or pain that we are being punished. Our flesh tells us that bad things happen to bad people. During my trials, I learned that in order to grow, I would experience growing pains. If I want to be the fastest track athlete, my conditioning will be painful, not only for my legs, but for my entire body. God was conditioning me to exercise patience, and it hurt! I now know that the more I exercise it, the stronger I will become in my season of wait. I discovered that over 9 years ago, and I still exercise longsuffering. The good thing is that the suffering will not last forever and that everyone embarks on different journeys.

A TASTE OF THE SPIRITUAL FRUIT

Love

Jesus is the perfect example of the fruit of the spirit. He endured a lot in His life and He felt the same emotions we feel. I encourage you to place yourself in Jesus' shoes and envision yourself on His journey. Jesus was a man who felt everything we feel, witnessed terrible things, endured various trials, and still exhibited all of character traits of the fruit of the spirit through His arrest, His trial, and even through His crucifixion. Jesus' greatest love was through His sacrifice and crucifixion.

Love is the first fruit of the spirit. Let's understand that Jesus loved us so much, even people who did not believe in His divine power, people who slandered Him, people who mocked and laughed at Him, and people who envied Him. Regardless, He sacrificed His power and glory to become a human being and be placed in situations where He was humiliated, suffered, and died all for us (Philippians 2:5-11). I do not know anyone who would make that much sacrifice for people who would mistreat them. That is an example of absolute and actionable love.

Joy

In all that Jesus experienced, He showed joy, which is the second fruit of the spirit. Jesus understood God's plan to "… bring many sons to glory" (Hebrews 2:10, KJV). No matter what cost He had to pay, pleasing His Father brought Him joy. That's deep! Wow, can we relate to that? This is a form of unselfish love. Can you imagine loving someone so much that you would do all you can to provide for them or to make them happy? You would be willing to put in work. Jesus knew that His work would please His Father, so He considered it joy, despite the challenge.

Hebrews (12:2) states, "…Jesus, the author and finisher of our faith; for the joy that was set before Him endured the cross, despising the shame, and has sat down at the right hand of the throne of God" (KJV). What I love about this scripture is that the joy was set in Him prior to enduring the cross. It's not something we can instantly acquire. As I mentioned before, spiritual fruit is work that is mustered in us. Because Jesus was already filled with joy, no matter what obstacles came His way, He was able to endure it with an optimistic mindset, and by showing gratitude towards His Father.

Peace

Peace is the third spiritual fruit, and it is something that many of us desire. With all of the problems we face and tasks we endure, peace is one of the first things we would order if it was on a menu. If only our doctors could prescribe us with a dose of peace! Isaiah (9:6) referenced Jesus as the "Prince of Peace" (KJV). Peace is something only God can give us. Many of us try to acquire peace through circumstances and in others. In John 14:27, Jesus told His disciples at the last supper, *"Peace I leave with you, My peace I give to you; not as the world gives so I give to you. Let not your heart be troubled, neither let it be afraid"* (ESV). Jesus' heart is so full of peace in the last hours of His life, that He offers words of encouragement to others. Knowing what He was about to endure through His faith, even in the midst of trouble, He had peace in His heart and carried out God's plan through His crucifixion.

Understand that we will endure some attacks in our lives, but the gift of peace will help us endure the pain, knowing that the peace we need is God's peace. If we believe that the world can give us peace, then we will allow the world to take it away. Know that anything God gives you cannot be taken away from you by the world when you are rooted in Him.

Longsuffering (Patience)

The fourth spiritual fruit is longsuffering, commonly known as patience and endurance. I struggled as I mentioned before with patience. Jesus demonstrated perfect patience. Jesus was a teacher and leader of His disciples. In many ways, He was their "personal trainer." As an educator, I understood what it was like to be patient with students when trying to get them to understand concepts. Some have different learning styles, learn at different speeds, or just do not have the desire to understand based on previous or current experiences. Regardless, what I taught were facts, and I provided a plethora of examples of how and why each concept makes sense in real life. However, each year, I came across that one student that no matter how I taught it, they refused to believe that they were capable of understanding the concept because they did not believe in themselves.

I could have done one of two things. I could have given up on them, or I could have been patient and continued to teach them the content as well as encourage them that they were capable of learning, despite what they believed. Jesus was a true example of a teacher who was patient even when disciples did not always trust His word. Many times, they allowed fear to settle in even after Jesus performed miracles before their very eyes. Jesus fed 5,000 people with only five loaves of bread and two fish (Matthew 14:15-21), allowed a mute man to speak (Matthew 9:32-33), healed the eyes of two blind men (Matthew 9:27-31), raised the synagogue leader's daughter from the dead (Matthew 9:18-26), quieted the storm with his disciples (Matthew 8:23-27), cured a demon-possessed man (Matthew 12:22), healed a withered hand (Matthew 12:10-13), cured a paralytic (Matthew 9:1-8), and He performed many more miracles. However, Jesus' disciples were still afraid when He appeared before them by walking on the water. They were troubled, saying, "It is a ghost!" (Matthew 14:26, NKJV). They cried out in fear.

> "But immediately Jesus spoke to them, saying, "Be of good cheer! It is I; do not be afraid." And Peter answered Him and said, "Lord, if it is You, command me to come to You on the water." So He said, "Come." And when Peter had come down out of the boat, he walked on the water to go to Jesus. But when he saw that the wind was boisterous, he was afraid; and beginning to sink he cried out, saying, "Lord, save me!" And immediately Jesus stretched out His hand and caught him, and said to him, "O you of little faith, why did you doubt?" And when they got into the boat, the wind ceased," (Matthew 14:27-32, NKJV).

I am quite sure there were many times Jesus could have just thrown in the towel. His love for them and patience with them, even during His trying times remained strong.

Kindness

Kindness is another character trait of Jesus and the fifth fruit of the spirit. Jesus not only had the ability to heal, but was kind enough to lend a healing hand to those in need without judging them. Various books throughout the bible states numerous miracles performed by Jesus' kind gestures. One in particular was Jesus healing a man who had leprosy. This terrible disease made him an outcast and untouchable to man, for he was considered to be unclean. Many of us would refuse to stand next to someone with a common cold or even offer them a Kleenex, because, we are more so selfishly looking after ourselves instead of offering help or comfort to those who are in need. However, Jesus saw that this man with leprosy had a need, and He made him clean with just a simple touch.

When was the last time you touched someone in a positive way? Were you there to listen to someone vent about their troubles even when you were in a rush to do other things? Have you stepped up to offer encouragement to someone who was ridiculed because their appearance was different or they displayed an awkward persona? Have you offered to help someone who was not so pleasant with you in the past? Did Jesus have to heal this man? No, but His love for God allowed Him to see beyond the scars on his skin and provoked an urge to heal him regardless.

Goodness

Have you ever heard of the statement, "God is good all the time. And all the time, God is good?" It is only because it is so true. Goodness is the next fruit of the spirit. One of God's greatest examples of goodness towards humanity is the sacrifice of His son, Jesus Christ. Among many more, Jesus exercised goodness throughout His life. When Jesus was preaching in Capernaum, a group of men tried to get near Him as He preached to a crowd of people. They wanted Jesus to heal their paralyzed friend. Because they could not get through the crowd, they made a hole in the roof above Jesus to get to Him, then lowered the paralyzed man towards Him on a mat. Let's just pause here to examine that they realized how important Jesus was that they made a way, regardless of how large the crowd was. Jesus saw that their faith in Him was so big, without any questioning, He told the men, "Your sins are forgiven" (Mark 2:5, NIV). Because his friends had faith in Him, Jesus demonstrated that man could too forgive each other, teaching us that we can be good to each other in that manner. Soon after, He healed the paralyzed man.

Goodness is nothing to take for granted. God has been so good to us by way of mercy that we sometimes expect God to save us even when we intentionally make wrong choices. God's love is unmerited. That's just how good He is. He will grant us favor and many blessings regardless of our economic status, popularity, credibility or work experience. Wouldn't it be nice to be treated that way by those around us? Through goodness, we too will be healed.

Faith

Walking in faith and not by sight is not always easy, especially when facing trials. Jesus' life depicts a true representation of His unwavering faith in God's plan. When looking at a timeline of disappointments and struggles Jesus encountered, He never gave up. Jesus experienced doubt from many people who did not agree with His teachings as well as abandonment from His disciples, whom He taught, counseled and performed miracles around. In addition, people turned their backs against Him, His disciples denied they knew Him, and He faced rejection from Jews. Then there were moments when He faced tremendous torture. He was imprisoned for loving His Father, whipped repeatedly until His skin tore, spat on, talked about, lied on, mocked, pierced through his feet and hands, ridiculed and placed on display in front of a crowd, and crucified on a cross. Through all of those frustrating moments, Jesus still believed God would fulfill His promise, and Jesus kept His faith. That is strength like no other.

Gentleness

Gentleness is the eighth fruit of the spirit. This is referenced as being meek and humble. Philippians 4:5 tells us to "let your gentleness be evident to all. The Lord is near" (NIV). There is a misconception that being gentle or humble is a sign of weakness. Jesus was very gentle; however, he was outspoken and assertive. He was not prideful nor arrogant although he was powerful. In John (13:2-10), Jesus washes the feet of His disciples hours before His crucifixion. Many people we know in authoritative roles delegate responsibilities. In the text, it is plain that Jesus partakes in servicing those who learn from Him. Paul questioned His behavior, but Jesus insisted on cleansing them and made it known in verse 8 that if He does not do this, they have no part in Him. He loved them so much that He humbled Himself to wash their feet so that they could remain in part with Him.

Self-Control

Self-control is the final fruit of the spirit. Exemplifying self-control is the ability to control one's behavior. Jesus was simply a perfect man who embodied all of God's spiritual fruit. He had self-control. He had so much of it, that He was able to put any desires of the flesh aside to please God. In Luke 22:42, Jesus prayed to His Father the night He was arrested. In His prayer, he said the following: "Father, if you are willing take this cup of suffering away from me. But do what you want, not what I want" (NIRV). Many would admit that we would ask for something called mercy. Our prayers are often more self-seeking and filled with promises. "Lord, if you deliver me, I promise I would..., or I promise I would not..." We are accustomed to asking for the desires of *our* hearts, but with self-control, we are able to seek the desires of *His* heart.

WORK IN PROGRESS

God's spiritual fruit can be everlasting if we take part in it daily. Each day I personally aim to grow to be an extension of Him. The work is not easy, but anything of good quality requires effort. God wants us to be fruitful and highly productive. If we really think about this, fruit is God's spiritual reference to what we produce in our lives through our relationships and experiences with God, not man. Colossians 1:9-12 states that fruitfulness is tied to the *knowledge* of God. Anyone can be successful, but without God's connection, success will not last long.

As I got older, I knew God was with me when I needed to make big decisions; however, as a young adult, my personal relationship with Him was part-time in some instances. I worked and traveled a lot throughout college and graduate school, so I did what many Christians may do, put God on the back burner to take care of other things. Is it ironic that we know God is the maker and ruler of all things-this entire world, but we prioritize other things before Him? Realistically, I know life gets hectic especially when there are bills to pay, jobs to go to, school to attend, children and family to feed, and even meetings to attend. They are all things that may be necessary to function and survive. If we spend our time doing only those things, then we are just tasking time away and may miss opportunities to build relationships with God and radiate His true character. He is what we need to function in life. Just as the human body needs food, water, and rest to survive, we need God.

The core is the foundation of any object or living thing and without it, it will cave in or perish. Understand that spiritual fruit, filtered through the Holy Spirit must be used to develop; therefore, we must be put in situations where we must use our fruit. In order for us to become whole, we must not be afraid to grow!

We are all a work in progress, but just as I stated earlier, if we ask for the fruit of the spirit to be developed in our lives, we must expect to encounter people that will be difficult to get along with. When temptations come, exercising our character will be a continuous cycle. Consciously submit to God and depend on Him solely. We must first learn how to exercise our core (spirit) by asking to receive God's spiritual gifts and exercise it as often as we can.

CHAPTER 3

EXERCISING LOVE

If I compared the word love to fruit, I would compare it to strawberries. Oh, how I love strawberries! They are romantic, sweet, can be dipped in chocolate, and are red and heart shaped, reminding me of love. Among many other benefits, strawberries are low in calories, contain fiber, magnesium, and vitamins C and K. Knowing that strawberries possess these benefits, we may notice at times, strawberries are not always cheap, especially the plump and luscious bunch.

An interesting fact about strawberries is that it is an accessory fruit, meaning that the fleshy part is not derived from plant ovaries. The seeds on the outside of the fruit comes from the ovaries of the flower. You may be thinking, what does this have to do with love. Well love, like strawberries is a special type of spiritual fruit. In Galatians 5:22-23, it is the first spiritual fruit mentioned. The bible states that God is love, so we must exemplify Him in that manner towards others. We must understand what love is to represent it properly.

What I like about the strawberry is that benefits do not only come from the fruit itself, but the leaves from the plant it grows from an be eaten, cooked or raw, and used to make tea. That is how love is-universal. 1 Corinthians 13:4-8 states that

"… love is patient and kind; love does not envy or boast; it is not arrogant or rude. It does not insist on its own way; it is not irritable or resentful; it does not rejoice at wrongdoing, but rejoices with the truth. Love bears all things, believes all things, hopes all things, endures all things…" (ESV).

Love is kind (verse 4), meaning all elements of you should represent love. It is not just one thing shown in just one way. It embodies kindness, patience, gentleness, self-control, faith- pretty much all components of God's spiritual fruit that are beneficial to us and others. Just like love, humans can receive benefits from not only the strawberry alone, but from the entire plant.

It's easy to reference love to good feelings, such as feeling safe, warm and fuzzy, happy, generous, and supported. That is the way it is appeared in this society. We treat love as an emotion or feeling that is often given based on what we can receive, rather than a part of who we are. For instance, we celebrate Valentine's Day, which is a day that is celebrated annually to celebrate romance or romantic love. Nice gesture; however, we have commercialized this holiday to the point where people respond to love in different ways. For Valentine's Day, either people feel forced to purchase something for their significant other, they count this date as the only day, besides an anniversary, birthday or Christmas to display love, or some singles may feel unloved because they may not have a significant other.

Love is much more than just being in a romantic relationship with someone or displaying love towards people we know. It is not dependent on feelings or emotions. Love is much deeper than that.

When we can do all things stated in 1 Corinthians 13:4-8 despite of how we feel, what we may be experiencing in our lives, and someone's actions towards and around us, then we exhibit love. True love occurs regardless, and expect nothing in return. In all that was stated earlier about love, there is no doubt that love is an action word. So how is love patient and kind? Let's delve into the parable of the unmerciful servant.

Parable of the Unmerciful Servant

In Matthew 18:21-36, Jesus told the story of a servant who owed a large debt to his master. At the time, he was unable to pay, so his master ordered he and his family to be sold into slavery to repay the debt. The servant begged for mercy, promising that he would pay back everything he owed if his master would be *patient* with him. His master pitied him, withdrew the order, and was kind enough to let the servant go. Thereafter, the servant found a fellow servant of *his* whom owed him money. This amount was less that the amount he owed his master. However, when he saw his servant, he choked him and demanded he pay him back what he owed.

Let's pause here. Does this story sound familiar? Have you ever been in a bind and needed more time to handle your responsibilities? Has someone helped you out? If yes, weren't you grateful at that moment? However, your period of gratefulness may have been a temporary emotion. Have you later charged someone else for their mistake and held them accountable for the same thing we received mercy for? In this parable, the servant's servant responded in verse 29, "...be patient with me, and I will pay it back" (NIV). It was the same words he asked of his master and interestingly so, he refused to be patient and threw the man into prison until he could pay off the debt. This is not what love should look like. As a consequence, his master was so furious of his actions after he was patient and loving towards his needs, he sent him to jail to be tortured until he was able to pay back his debt. Unless we forgive our brothers and sisters genuinely, we will see God's wrath.

1 Corinthians 13:4-8 provided several examples of what love is not. Love is not self-seeking. Selfless love is unfortunately rare. It is common to assume that when someone is suddenly nice to us, there is a motive behind it, and vice versa. It is possibly because we do not make ourselves available to others the way we should because we live busy lives, or that we have experienced people with motives in the past.

An example of unselfish love is the love a parent has for his/her child. Many good parents would do all they could to provide for their children without expecting anything back in return. We want to naturally make them happy and not boast or receive profit from our efforts, but genuinely make them feel safe. God is like that towards us. He only wants good for us and would do all He could to provide that to us.

John 15:13 states, "Greater love has no one than this, than to lay down one's life for his friends" (NKJV). The sacrifice of His Son, Jesus Christ is a true example of selfless love. Be honest, could you sacrifice your child for someone else's sins. Could you even *be* the sacrifice? I stated earlier that in each example I provide for you to place yourself in each situation. Selfless love is not something that molds into your character overnight. It takes time to develop, but when it does, it is so pure.

King Soloman and the Baby

In 1 Kings 3:16-28, King Soloman was faced with a difficult decision. A mother from the story demonstrated a pure heart when she sacrificed her bond with her child to spare his life. I watch many Lifetime movies, so I have seen many pictures of women trying to steal newborns from other women. Can you imagine yourself discovering you were pregnant one day and filled with excitement about the gift God birthed within you? You endured a nine-month pregnancy with high emotions and anxiety of the arrival of your precious child. You endured labor pains, a delivery, and finally an immediate bond with your first born. After this entire experience, you found out your roommate tried to steal your baby! How would you feel? I'm quite sure your maternal instincts within you would fight for your child. This woman experienced the very same thing. Her roommate had a baby she accidentally killed by rolling over him. To cover her mistake, she took her dead baby and exchanged it with her roommate's baby. How crazy is that?

The next day, the woman discovered that the dead baby was not her own, so she and the dishonest woman argued both claiming the alive child as their own. They both took the child to King Soloman to plead their cases. His response was to cut the baby in half so that each mother could have a part of him.

The foul woman did not hesitate, encouraging the King to cut the baby, while the maternal mother of the child resisted and begged the king not to harm the baby. The other woman felt that since her baby died, they both did not deserve a child. The real mother's actions showed that her unselfish love for her child is so pure that she was able to put her competitive feelings aside and give up her child to the unfit mother to prevent him from dying.

Knowing that if the King allowed the other woman to raise her child, she would experience a time of emptiness and sadness, but she put her pride aside, being a true example of what selfless love looks like. It was her actions, not her words that lead King Soloman to make the decision to give the child to the maternal mother. When we remember that love is an action word, we will learn that love is something that must be demonstrated, not simply spoken.

LOVE THROUGH PAIN

Putting our own feelings aside can be quite difficult at times. For example, I find it unfortunate to hear about parents who share children together fight an ugly fight for custodial rights for their children after the demise of their relationship. Sometimes, a custody battle can be a beast because the competitive nature between both parents may lead them towards making irrational and selfish decisions. The best interest of the child at times is no longer an interest, and motives to destroy and hurt each other becomes self-seeking.

As a mother, I know what it is like to love a child unconditionally. I have experienced a custody battle for my only child. It stemmed from a relationship I no longer wanted to take part in. I must admit, that it was the best thing I could have done at that time. I was unsure of what my future looked like, and my finances were not in spectacular order, but I tried my best not to worry. Despite this, I did all I could to ensure my child received everything he needed.

Was it an easy journey? Not at all, but when needing to practically start all over, care for someone with all of your heart, and learn this political game called "custody battle", my child deserved to receive nothing short of love.

Was it an easy journey? Not at all, but when needing to practically start all over, care for someone with all of your heart, learn this political game called "custody battle", all while being provoked and defamed, my child deserved to receive nothing short of love.

Love also does not envy, thinks no evil, and does not boast. We are a part of a commercial driven society where everyone is advertising a product for consumers to purchase. It seems each time we turn on the television, we see enhanced beauty, vacation advertisements, luxury vehicles, expensive homes, and happy families all laced with reality shows along with a dose of social media. Because of this, we compete and covet.

If you don't believe me, then answer this question. How would you treat people if things in your life were unfair? What if someone at your job was an incompetent worker that you always assisted when they were in need. Suddenly, you both apply for a promotion that you feel should fall in your lap; however, your co-worker received it instead of you? Would your actions towards him or her change? Would you feel envious of them? Would evil thoughts form in your mind? Would you be too proud to help them? What if your best friend was a terrible girlfriend? She always cause drama in relationships and has a selfish attitude, but the good men seem to be attracted to her. You know, the fine men that are your type. You know you are a good woman and you would love it if a nice man just fell in your lap, but your opportunity has not yet come. Would you still offer her relationship advice although in your mind, you may feel like since she ruined several other good relationships, she does not deserve it?

Sometimes, without even realizing it, we develop feelings such as these and respond out of spite towards people suddenly. These are not loving behaviors. Godly love finds contentment no matter what happens. When jealousy and envy arise, it represents signs of discontentment of what we may or may not have, or who we are. Envy is a dangerous emotion that could cause harm to others and ourselves. An example of how envy can harm us is in 1 Samuel 18.

The Story of Saul and David

King Saul was a man plagued by an evil spirit. His disobedience to God caused him to lose his thrown to David, a favored and wise man. King Saul, an accomplished and competent military leader developed anger and envy in his heart towards David and did all he could to try to destroy him. Prior to him losing his thrown, David was a great help to him by helping him defeat Israel's enemy. However, King Saul took pride in receiving credit for great things happening under his reign.

After Israel's enemy was defeated, excited women from the towns of Israel came out to meet them singing and dancing, saying, "…Saul has slain his thousands and David his tens of thousands…" (1 Samuel 18:7, NIV). It angered Saul to see that David received more credit. Thereafter, Saul kept a watchful eye on David, watching people closest to him favor David. His hatred towards him continued to grow, and because of this, Saul became David's enemy.

This story is an example of how hatred, envy, and jealousy, contrary to love, can cause blindness. David was a person of potential, power, and favor that Saul could have benefitted from. His inability to let his pride down blocked him from many blessings that could have come his way. Note that although King Saul was a competent leader, it was not by his might. Philippians 4:13 reads, "I can do all things through Christ who strengthens me" (NKJV). Once you lose connections with God and make no attempt to partake of His fruit, you will soon understand that what you once had could definitely be taken away.

Love is so powerful, it never fails, EVER. So, what does this mean? It means love never ends. We see the word fail, and feel like when marriages, friendships, and relationships with relatives fail that all is lost and we can no longer offer love to that person. Love is often difficult for us because we want to control how people receive it and what others may do in return. Think about it. If we put more effort towards a marriage, and our spouse is not pulling their weight, we want to give up, because the love we put towards it is no longer reciprocated. Going back to 1 Corinthians 13:5, love is not self-seeking. Loving ourselves is easy, because we can control us, and we know what we want. Loving others is challenging because we cannot control the actions of others.

Love is actionable to others, not ourselves. When we do things for others, it should be from the goodness of our hearts- even when it is not received in a way we expect it to be received. In all we do and no matter what, we should show love and never stop at trying to show case it. Love is also a word that has no conditions; therefore, it does not fluctuate. We could probably count several conditions we place in our marriages, relationships, and friendships. If love encompass several traits of the spiritual fruit, there should be no limitations to whom you love and how you love them.

Parable of the Prodigal Son

Love sounds simple until we are tested to love those who are unkind to us whether they are related to us or not. This reminds me of the parable of the Prodigal Son. In Luke 15:11-32, this parable is about a father and two sons. The older son was a model child whom did everything his father asked, was hard working, and very responsible with his earnings. The younger son exhibited different characteristics contrary to his brother. He was lazy and very selfish. He wanted his share of his father's estate so that he could squander his wealth in wild living.

Soon after, he wasted everything he had, then realized that even his father's servants worked so hard, they had food to spare. He desired that, so he ran off to tell his father to make him like one of his hired servants, and apologized for sinning the way he did.

This pleased his father. To celebrate, his father placed his best robe on him, placed a ring on his finger, sandals on his feet, and then killed the fattest calf so they could have a feast to celebrate. When the older son heard of this, he was angered. He confronted his father, expressing to him how unfair this situation was that he was always obedient, responsible, and hardworking and was never celebrated for all of his efforts, but the one time his brother realized the error of his ways, a huge feast was thrown.

He felt that this was unfair. His father; however, reassured his son that everything he had was his, but in that moment, he needed to celebrate the fact that his dead brother has come back to life, for he was lost and is now found. Many of us can totally relate to this because as I stated before, when things in life are unfair, our attitudes towards others change.

There are two messages here. First of all, the older brother, although in his feelings, should have been happy that his younger brother had a breakthrough. He was focused on the excitement and commotion and not thinking about his change. When we truly love someone, we should not place conditions on our love towards them. Would you want God to keep record of your wrongs and then place conditions on how He treats us? We all make mistakes, but it is not our place to judge others in a way where we feel like they are beneath us.

Second, our love should affect others. Imagine if his father responded to him in a way that was condescending, cruel, or simply unloving. He could have easily said, "Well son, I regret it has taken you this long to come to your senses. You have been irresponsible and wicked in your ways." You know, tell him everything he already knows. We have the tendency to do that at times, not realizing that we make more of a contribution towards hurt rather than help.

Now, I am an advocate of showing tough love, but this parable shows us a clear picture of how quickly we get into attack mode when people around us receive good treatment during unfair situations. We want to be careful not to run people away when they are trying to make better decisions.

LEARNING HOW TO LOVE

Learning how to love can be tricky, because some people may misinterpret components of love by thinking they can be in abusive relationships with people because love does not discriminate. In every decision we make, we must ask God for wisdom and guidance. Have you heard of the expression, birds of a feather flock together? If you surround yourself with people who will destroy you instead of build you up, then you will experience disappointment. Proverbs 13:20 states, "Whoever walks with the wise will become wiser; for a companion with fools suffers harm" (NIV). Take heed to intuitive signs God gives us. We often struggle with hurt because we have yet to discover what we love. Most importantly, many people have not taken the time to love themselves. I can't say I'm a good wife if I do not know what the role of a wife is. It's impossible to rate without knowing. The same applies to love. We can't say we love ourselves if we don't know who we are.

God never intended for us dwell in toxic relationships with people in our lives who continuously bring us down rather than uplift us. When we are not cognizant of our worth, we allow our value to fall to a low setting. The more we learn to love ourselves, we allow our value meter to break through the glass ceiling. Knowing who we are is important when learning how to interact with others. When we know what love does not look like and what we don't like, we are less likely to be blinded by society's interpretation of love through *emotions*.

I spoke on several components of love, but loving your enemies is by far one of the toughest components of love for me. Have you ever thought about this? How can you love someone who plotted against you, tried to steal from you, defamed you, looked down upon you, used you, broke your heart, etc...? I can go on and on. Believe it or not, there are people on this Earth who have endured deep trials. Some people may have been convicted and served time in prison under false accusations and still forgave their accuser- whether they received an apology or not. Some people lost loved ones by the hands of people in a fit of rage or hate and have forgiven them in their hearts- whether the abuser was remorseful or not.

Love can be shown in so ways. Many people have a difficult time praying for those who have hurt their loved ones or themselves. We wonder how can we pray for God to heal them, especially when we want to feel vindicated? Take a moment to think about someone in your life that you consider your enemy, or whom you had a difficult time forgiving. In some cases, you may not have even known someone envied you at some point, but for some reason, they love to test your temperament. Now think about how you have responded to them in the past. Was it loving? Was it a reaction? In Matthew 5:43-48, Jesus said the following, "But I say to you, love your enemies and pray for those who persecute you, so that you may be sons of your Father who is in heaven… For if you love those who love you, what reward do you have..." (ESV).

Love is about healing. It's medicine we take in and distribute to others. I shared an example with my son about loving your enemies. I compared how to express love to people who experience pain and need healing. I explained that if he experienced an accident, such as twisting his ankle, I would take him to the emergency room so that the doctor could determine the seriousness of the injury and help alleviate the pain.

We've been in an emergency room before, and although it's for emergencies, many patients are not immediately seen by anyone. The wait time could take hours. I continued to tell him that if in the middle of our wait someone is rushed in with gunshot wounds in their flesh, a doctor would immediately treat them. My inquisitive son interrupted me with a question and asked, "Mommy, that's not fair. Why should they get seen before me if my ankle is hurting and swollen?" I responded, "Well, the person who was shot was in a worse condition. They need more attention than everyone else. They are in a position where the health risk is higher than yours and they are in need of an invasive procedure by someone who specializes in healing. I asked, "Would you want to wait in line to see the doctor if your life was in jeopardy?"

My son received my point. In our society, we are accustomed to doing things in a particular order. We wait in lines at drive thru windows, in traffic, at supermarkets, etc… We simply wait our turn, but in an order. It's easy to plan for something to happen because in the physical, we were next in line, but God has an order that may not make sense to us, but is perfect. So when referring to loving our enemies, it's easy to compare who you are to them and decide that blessings should come to us first because we have faith and live according to God's word.

But, those who are not rooted in the word nor live by the will of God need more love than any saint because they lack the mental and spiritual capacity to survive without it. They need to be saved!

God is a healer. It is hard to heal those who are not sick. Notice that Satan doesn't bother the sick, but he comes after the strong. Although we are waiting in emergency rooms with swollen ankles, dislocated shoulders, and migraine headaches, regardless of the character of the person who was rushed in shot, their need in the moment is much greater than ours. Because God wants us to live in harmony, we must exercise love towards others even when it hurts.

Poor treatment is hurtful, both ways. Naturally, when we hurt, we want those who hurt us to feel the same way, or worse. Understand that hurt people hurt people. As much as it hurts, God does not want us to behave in any way that will allow us to become the type of person we do not want others to treat us as.

You see, this is a difficult function of love that is not exercised often. Our spirit is constantly wrestling against the flesh, and it is often a tug of war. Our flesh wants to lash out and vindicate everything, but the spirit is telling us that we do not have to fight every battle. We fight fire with fire and cry when we get burned. Now that hurts even more.

In Proverbs, we are advised to kill our enemies with kindness; however, in all we do, be wise. "If your enemy is hungry, give him food to eat; if he is thirsty, give him water to drink. In doing this, you will heap burning coals on his head, and the LORD will reward you" (Proverbs 25:21-22, NIV). We must be careful not to allow our actions with others to minimize our character, stooping us to their level. The bible teaches us to be the change God wants to see and by doing so, He will reward us. Each day we dispense the medication of love towards others, God will give us a double portion of His.

Have you ever been bullied by someone? Many people who bully others lack confidence, have low self-esteem, or need to do something to make them feel superior to others to compensate for qualities they may lack. If you have experienced a bully, have you tried to turn the other cheek? Matthew 5:44-45 states, "But I say to you, love your enemies, bless those who curse you, do good to those who hate you, and pray for those who spitefully use you and persecute you, that you may be sons of your Father in heaven" (NKJV). Now, I am not saying we should give gifts to our enemies after they wore us down emotionally. In all that we do, we should be wise.

The scripture is saying that we should display good character before them. I understand we must be assertive and stand up for ourselves. I am not implying that you should not. As I stated in Chapter 2, Jesus was gentle and kind; however, He was outspoken and assertive. What made Him so great was that He knew the word, was fearless and His faith in God was *uncompromising*. What we witnessed from Him was the real deal. *His buttons could not be pushed*; therefore, the reaction enemies wanted from Him were not given unto them.

In many cases, if we entertain the antics of bullies, we become their long-term bait. Then, we will have a bigger problem on our hands. When we give them everything but what they desire, confusion surfaces in their space, not ours.

I must caution you before I explore into love a bit more. When we try to exemplify all of the aforementioned components of love, expect to be tempted by others. This is how we condition ourselves to show these types of love and grow. The journey to the Kingdom is not always a pleasant ride. Jesus' journey as a perfect man was far from that. So what makes us as sinners think our journey should be better? The enemy will do all he can to provoke us; therefore, it is important to live a balanced life.

The Apostle Paul was provoked in judgement when he observed a city filled with idols (Acts 17:16). He was frustrated with the crowd's behavior, but he was able to rejoice in the truth by continuing to spread the good news about Jesus and the resurrection regardless of any outbursts received from the crowds. His love for God and the sake of others allowed him to share the good news even though he received backlash. Had the Apostle Paul not loved God wholeheartedly, it would have been easy for him to give up on the crowd when they rose against him. However, his mission was not to please himself, it was to please God.

Love can be a tricky action when we love for the wrong reasons. When we do, expect the unchanged ex-boyfriend or ex-girlfriend who mistreated you to find a place back into your life. When we love from our flesh and not our spirit, it's easy to be fooled by the deceiver then find ourselves repeating an emotional cycle of disappointment. Again, we do not have to be best friends with everyone, especially those who have caused us pain and has not matured since. It is okay to show love from a distance, and know that through separation there is a purpose.

UNWRAPPING LOVE

Are we capable of showing Godly love? Can we forgive the heartless murderer who took the life of our loved one for no reason at all? Can we be loving towards the now remorseful individual who killed our family member in a car accident because he or she was intoxicated? How can we show Godly love to others if someone wrongfully accused us of a crime that resulted in a twenty-year prison sentence all to find out the justice system made a mistake after our release? How can we be happy for others who celebrate the life of a child when we have made failed attempts to conceive? We are far from perfect and no one lives perfect lives, but we are allowed opportunities to attempt to show Godly love each day. Love is action often made in sacrifices. The pursuit of exemplifying Godly love requires sacrificing our feelings, time and our energy.

Lastly, "Above all, love each other deeply, because love covers a multitude of sins" (I Peter 4:8, NIV). Some of us find it difficult to even love our own relatives, so loving all people seems impossible. But God says it is. You may have thought that it was impossible to eat strawberry leaves or that there were no health benefits of taking all that the plant could offer. I have good news, it is possible, and it is also possible to attempt to love everyone in every way God expects us to. Once we understand what is required of us, then we can love holistically. "If someone says, 'I love God' and hates his brother, he is a liar; for he who does not love his brother who he has seen, how can he love God whom he has not seen? And this commandment we have from Him. That he who loves God must love his brother" (1 John 4:20-21, NKJV). Remember, love is actionable, not verbiage.

WE EXERCISE LOVE WHEN:

- We are able to forgive.
- Our actions do not harm others.
- We pray for others, even those who have wronged us.
- We can warn people of their actions without casting judgement on them.
- We can help someone in need.
- We willingly share a testimony about how God has helped and delivered us.
- We can put aside our feelings for the benefit of others.

What I love about 1 Corinthians 13:4-8 is that it lists what love is and what love is not. In order to grow in love, it is necessary for us to assess our actions each day by comparing them to the scripture. I am actually growing in love. As a newlywed, I now see love at an entirely different capacity. Trust me when I say that it isn't easy! We have endured immediate trials after we said, "I do." But as I mentioned before, the enemy wants to destroy what he's intimidated by. So instead, I fight back, but against the enemy and not my husband.

God is so good, even when we feel things in our lives are so unfair. When we experience trials, being loving may seem to be the hardest thing to do. Understand that before any trials, we know *of* God. During the trials, He conditions us to *understand* more about Him. But after the storm, *we know God*. By knowing God, we can trust His will and allow Him to help us surrender to love.

CHAPTER 4

EXERCISING JOY

When I hear the word joy, I immediately think of the sound of Lauryn Hill in Sister Act 2, singing "Joyful, Joyful". The sound of her amazing voice brings chills to my bones. Beyond her voice are the lyrics to the song: *"Joyful, Joyful, Lord, we adore Thee, God of glory Lord of love. Hearts unfold like flowers before Thee. Hail Thee as the sun above. Melt the clouds of sin and sadness. Drive the dark doubt away. Giver of immortal gladness.....fill us with the light of day..."* (Van Dyke, 1907). This is a song that speaks light to many. I encourage you to listen to this song if you are feeling down. This song is a great mode of encouragement referenced through joy.

We will experience joy when we believe that God is truly a giver of immortal gladness. Only He can melt away sin and sadness and drive doubt so far away that we no longer have access to it. If God is willing to do all of this, then I ask this question, *"What have you done for Him lately? Ooh, ooh, ooh, yeah!..."*

Joy is the second fruit of the spirit. If I compared joy to an actual fruit, I would compare it to an orange. Oranges are bright, juicy and sweet, is a great source of vitamin C, and carry a great scent. Just one medium orange provides the recommended daily amount of vitamin C for adults. The vitamin C found in oranges helps build the immune system so that common colds, the flu, and coughs are no longer a threat.

Oranges can be used to make fresh orange juice, to cook with, and to add to beverages to provide flavor. Children even like to shove orange halves into their mouths playfully to show orange teeth. What I love about them is that they are easy to pack. I can throw one in my bag without any preparation needed. So are you packing joy in your bag each day? Let's find out what joy is and what joy is not.

"This is the day the Lord has made. Let us rejoice and be glad in it" (Psalm 118:24, ESV). This scripture is one many of us may have heard of before. Do we really understand it? It does not apply to rejoicing one day out of the week, or just when we encounter a happy moment in our lives. It refers to each day God blessed us with life. So no matter what doors were closed before us or what trials we may endure, we must find joy in this day and be grateful for the mercy God has on us.

There is always something to be grateful for, even when we do not believe it. A common misconception many people have is that joy and happiness are interrelated. That is not completely true. You may find happiness listed as a synonym of joy in the dictionary, but keep in mind that when pertaining to spiritual fruit, we are seeking edification through God's vision.

WHAT IS JOY?

The difference between happiness and joy is that happiness is an emotion and joy is not. Happiness comes and goes. Think about someone or something that made you happy. Maybe you encountered a new love companion or purchased a new home. Maybe you enjoyed happy hour after work, or simply binge watched your favorite movies eating ice cream. Circumstances, big or small, makes us happy. In those examples, happiness occurred based on how you felt about someone or something at that time. But, if your date turned out to be a nightmare, would you still be happy with him or her? If you gained three pounds from the ice-cream you ate, would you be happy about that?

In life, there will be ups and downs. Because of this, God never intended for us to be in a state of happiness at all times. In Ecclesiastes

3:4, it states that there is "…a time to weep and a time to laugh, a time to mourn and a time to dance…" (KJV). When we are weeping and mourning, we are typically not happy. However, we can be joyful. How can that be? Well, joy is evidence of the presence of God in our lives. When we can endure heartbreak, loss, disappointment, or poor health, we can only have joy when God is connected to us.

We would be living a lie if we said we would be happy if our home foreclosed, or if we got fired from our job. Those things do not bring happiness to us, but in all things we encounter we can repair the damage with a joyful heart knowing that things can get better. In summary of Ecclesiastes 3, there is a time for everything, and through everything we encounter, God desires us to be joyful.

The Apostle Paul

I like to view joy from this perspective: what can we gain from being mad, bitter, or depressed. Refer back to the story of King Saul and David. Note that King Saul's lack of contentment and angered heart cost him his thrown and relationships. We can also ask ourselves, "What can we lose by being joyful?" Yes, it is so hard to not focus on what we consistently see or have to live through. But the bible says that joy transforms difficult circumstances into ties of blessings. 1 Peter 1:6-8 states:

"In this you greatly rejoice, though now for a little while, if need be, you have been grieved by various trials, that the genuineness of your faith, being much more precious than gold that perishes, though it is tested by fire, may be found to praise, honor, and glory at the revelation of Jesus Christ, whom having not seen you love" (NKJV).

The Apostle Paul's life is a considerable example of someone enduring various trials but remaining joyful, faithful, and encouraged. We think we have it bad in some instances, but in comparison to The Apostle Paul, we may have not endured much.

In 2 Corinthians 11, Paul speaks about his many trials. This man experienced imprisonment, multiple beatings and whippings, was stoned, shipwrecked multiple times, lived with a lack of food and water, faced danger and threats from his own people, was abandoned, and to top it all, he was given a thorn in his flesh, a messenger from Satan to torment him. Can you imagine enduring all of the physical pain he experienced and later being tormented emotionally by Satan? It would not surprise me if he was an emotional wreck. That is a lot to deal with. In fact it was so much that Paul begged the Lord to take it away (2 Corinthians 12:8).

Have any of you experienced moments that were so uncomfortable that you begged God to remove you from the situation- especially in your season of wait? Understand that he too was a human with real emotions. However, the Lord later responded that instead of simply removing the thorn that God's grace was sufficient. He was reassured that God's power works best in weakness (verse 9). So basically, God was not finished with teaching Paul a lesson. Knowing this, Paul rejoiced and boasted how he took delight in weakness, because when he is weak, God is strong. If God told us that, many of us would think we are being punished and only consider ourselves through our difficulties and discomfort.

By far, the Apostle Paul was not happy to endure the physical near death experiences and torture. It did not feel good. However, Paul was content with joy in knowing that he suffers for Christ so that Christ can work through him. In the scriptures, he states, "…For when I am weak, then I am strong" (2 Corinthians 12:10, NIV). A joyful spirit takes time to develop because it embodies several traits such as faith, gratefulness, hope, and a positive outlook on God's word. Because many of us approach life with a backwards perspective to things by walking by sight and not by faith, we often find it hard to see the big picture.

We are human. Therefore, it's okay to have feelings. There may be days when we feel defeated. We may experience long periods of wait. We may suffer through various trials or lose loved ones. We can cry, we can scream, we can vent to someone we trust, we can get angry…. it's okay. Once we release all of those built up emotions, then we'll see how our body reacts when some of that emotional weight is lifted from our thoughts.

I remember a point in time when I had headaches each evening at a consistent time. I was experiencing lows in my personal life and felt as if my body was getting ill. For the first two days, I did nothing. I just crawled into bed and tried to sleep away the pain. I am a person who rarely takes medication, so I had no relief. The following day, I had the same headache and began to feel sleepy; however, I had a ton of work to do within a 24-hour timeframe. My anxiety rose. Due to long-term stress, my health was not in the best state and I've intended to exercise more, but never had the time to. When I did, I had no desire to.

That day, I decided to, with a headache and all, run sprints down the trail in my neighborhood. Exercise makes me feel good, and as odd as it sounds, I exercised with my headache while my son rode his bike next to me. When I got home, my body felt weak for about 15 minutes, but when my heartrate returned to normal, to my surprise, my headache went away and I was able to complete my work related task. I wonder if I had concentrated on the "stuff" I had to do and not release that energy into a quick run, I would have probably invited an illness into my body, which would have been a new ailment. Sometimes in life, our problems may not immediately change, as in my situation, but the migraines (feelings/ emotions) always go away.

I know that emotions come and go, but the beauty of joy is that it lingers. A joyful person is not one who is perfect. They just have hope, which keeps them within God's reach. When we decide to no longer believe in God, then we continue to walk in the darkness. Have you ever walked in a dark room you've never seen before? The room is your future and darkness is unbelief. You do not know who or what is in the room (your future), but you choose to walk in it and get upset when you bump into a table or hit your toe on an object. Some may walk on snakes, into a furnace, get robbed, or find yourselves engulfed in the wrong crowd. Nevertheless, that's what life is like when we lack faith in God.

When we exercise faith, we produce joy. Romans 15:13 states, "May the God of hope fill you with all joy and peace in believing, so that by the power of the Holy Spirit you may abound in hope" (ESV). Hope will allow us to persevere. I compare this to toddlers when trying to walk. They believe that although they need to hold on to the edge of a table (God) to balance, they can walk like others. Because they have hope, regardless of how many times they fall, they will continue to try knowing the support (God) they have will help them through. Even if they can't walk independently the same day they practiced, regardless of how many times they cried, they are still joyful and will continue to try again on tomorrow. We do not physically know what our future looks like, but with God, we are able to walk into a future that is bright rather than dark.

Mary and Martha

Throughout my life, I have heard several references to joy. They are joy, unspeakable joy; cries of joy; rejoice in the Lord; shout for joy; the devil can't steal my joy; and (Psalm 30:5) "…weeping may stay for the night, but joy comes in the morning" (AMPC). We hear it, speak it, and sing it, but do we actually know what it is? If we do, do we believe joy exists?

Joy is largely composed of gratitude for the many great things God has done for us, and His promises made unto us. Joy is also tied to hope and faith. Romans 15:13 states, "May the God of hope fill you with all joy and peace in believing, so that the power of the Holy Spirit you may abound in hope" (ESV). Unfortunately, we do not see many examples of joy in this world. Instead, we see fear, worry, depression and hatred. It's sad, because from the time we open our eyes each day to the moment we close them at night, we are rushing through complicated lifestyles filled with tasks, responsibilities, and work. Our to do lists become our main focus, even if they are repetitive tasks each day. Because we put pressure on ourselves and receive it from others, it is very rare we stop to literally smell the roses. Because of this, our hope and peace diminish because our focus is on assignments created by man rather than those ordained to us by God.

This reminds me of the story of Martha and Mary. In Luke 10:38-42, Jesus and His disciples were coming to the home of Martha and

Mary. When they arrived, Mary was so intrigued by Jesus, she sat at His feet to listen to what He needed to say. She was actually present at His presence, allowing her undivided attention to remain on Him. Meanwhile, Martha, who greeted Him at the door, became distracted by all of her preparations. As she was busy tasking along, she noticed Mary *enjoying* Jesus' company. Martha became upset and asked Jesus to ask Mary to help her. She felt it was unfair that she is doing all of this work by herself.

Does this sound familiar to you? First of all, if you are doing things from the goodness of your heart, you should not seek credit. Second, Martha failed to realize that Jesus was gentle and humble. Although honorable, He was not impressed by a huge display. Third, Martha did not show that Jesus was important enough to engage in Him.

In verse 42, Jesus stated "…but few things are needed-or indeed only one" (NIV). Have you ever treated someone like this, but did not realize it? Can you imagine you came to visit a friend or relative you have not seen in a long time, and throughout the entire visit, they are mopping floors, washing dishes, checking email, studying, or typing a report? You my feel like you interrupted their space, or that they are not excited to see you because they have yet to engage with you. I must admit, I have inadvertently behaved like this at times. People would speak to me or try to converse with me as I am working or even concentrating on something, and I would respond without even looking at them because I was focused on my work. It is often very unintentional, but regardless, my focus was off and it became habitual. If only I stopped to think of the type of energy was I sending to people. Instead of taking a minute or two to just slow down and enjoy a conversation, I hid behind work that never went away.

I later realized that when I slowed down and enjoyed what was in front of me, the work that I thought was so pressing eventually went away on it's own. God then began to shift deadlines to accommodate the space I was in because I made more time for Him, and less time for work. Because Martha did not have joy in her heart, she missed an awesome experience with Jesus. Mary, contrary to Martha had so much joy in her life that she did not feel convicted by her actions. She was simply content, delighted and free.

Sometimes we have to just enjoy the moment. Have you heard of the expression, *"Are you living or existing?"* When we live, we are able to be free, enjoy the fruit of the Earth, and grow in Christ. When we exist, we are just there, nonproductive, and taking up space.

PRODUCING JOY

When was the last time you sat outside and enjoyed the fresh air? How often do you have a working lunch at work, or text or call someone to simply tell them you love them? When was the last time you had dinner with your family and intentionally ate at the table and held conversations with them to see how their day was? I remember moments when I was a child my mom cooked breakfast. I was never a breakfast eater, but she actually took time to cook a morning meal before we were sent off to school. I was not a "morning" person and would rather the extra sleep instead of sitting to eat breakfast. I now understand the value in her actions. If we can not set aside time for ourselves and loved ones in the comfort of our own homes, then is it likely we are setting time aside for God, someone we have not seen?

My point is that we experience joy when we are content with what God is doing for us and what He promised us. It is not a feeling that depends on a mood or emotion, it is a strong foundation of gratitude, optimism and freedom. If we are not careful, we can allow our busy schedules to suck the life out of us, because our focus is on the tasks, not enjoying the moment.

With social media and the Internet being a distraction, we often do not engage each other directly or even spend time alone with God. It is like trying to commit to exercising each day, but never allowing ourselves the time to do so. After a while, we find our health deteriorating to a worse condition than it was prior to the moment we decided we would commit to exercising. That is how we get spiritually. Our spiritual health is very important. If we ever spent time apart from God, we may find ourselves yearning for Him, needing Him, desiring Him, just as our bodies need water to survive. We must set time aside for God, each other, and ourselves. Today's news on social media and the Internet will be yesterday's news within seconds. So is it that important?

To grow in joy we must be planted sternly. Galatians 5 states that God's Spirit is a tree of life, producing life-giving fruit. The fruit includes great joy. If our structure (Holy Spirit) is not taken care of, we will not produce quality fruit.

When joy is firmly planted in our way of thinking, responding, and giving according to the will of God, we develop strong roots. Anytime a seed is sowed, the harvest takes time. I can't go to the store, purchase orange tree seeds, plant them and expect a tree full of oranges next month. This is how we behave at times. We reach a place of happiness in our lives and because we feel good, we think our character is good. We do nice things for people, walk around with smiles on our faces complimenting folks, and are even willing to be helpful.

Let's say we wanted to develop some joy. We go to church, read scriptures, and try to look at the world with an optimistic point of view. However, when God tests us by placing us in uncomfortable situations and we fail, we give up on this thing called joy. When the first sign of doubt and disappointment enter our lives, we find ourselves acting out of character, angry at the world, frowned, and no longer willing to help others because things appear to be unfavorable in our lives. Unfortunately, when we do not receive the things we want immediately, we crash. So, understand it takes time for joy to develop. God knows that the only way to get strong at anything is through exercise. When we can remain at peace during our storms and ride it out, we become strong.

Joy is something that is not self-centered. It must infect others around us. The orange I referenced has full benefits, like the strawberry. The peelings can give off a citrus aroma when boiled in hot water. If we run out of air freshener, orange peels are a great substitute. The aroma from the orange peels in just one pot delivers a soothing smell throughout the entire home, and it lasts a long time. When we are able to resist self-pity and transform our way of thinking from being self-seeking to serving others and God, we will experience long-lasting joy. Because joy is largely composed of gratitude for wonderful things God has done for us, we must be intentional about counting our blessings, especially during difficult times. When experiencing trials, our feelings are hurt. Proverbs 17:22 states, "A joyful heart is good medicine, but a crushed spirit dries up the bones" (ESV). Consider a dose of joy to help jumpstart your day. Just as the orange peels permeates an entire house with its aroma, allow joy to affect everyone you meet.

UNWRAPPING JOY

We are more than capable to produce joy in our spirits. Is it easy? Not always. When we experience pain, will be able to cope? If we are down on our luck, are we still optimistic God will fulfill His promise? When the storms in our lives cause devastation, would we be able to persevere to rebuild what was lost? Know that all is not lost if we stay connected to God. Tangible things, people, and temperament come and go. No matter what or whom we lose, we will always have a great gain when we hold on to God.

WE EXERCISE JOY WHEN:

- We no longer allow circumstances to waver our faith.
- We worry less and trust God even when things do not make sense, we release the anxiety and fear making our load light and our experiences enJOYable.
- We can focus on loving others and God.
- We are content with giving and serving rather than receiving.
- We are able to be optimistic and grateful for all God has done for us, is doing for us, and will do for us.
- When we learn to love regardless, we invite joy into our lives.

When we learn to love regardless, we invite joy into our lives. Love gets lost when we focus on tasks. Forward that energy towards God and be a blessing to others. We don't have to be in the best place in our lives to care about others. Care begins wherever we are and in whatever situation we are in.

It's easy to focus on repairing things in our lives we may find to be broken. But we're no professionals at repair. God is. Allow God to step in and resolve the issues. Our Father knows best. When we focus less on me, me, me or I, I, I, and allow God to handle it, we can focus on using gifts God blessed us with to be better examples for others. We will then learn that giving gives us more pleasure than receiving.

When we feel we interviewed well and that a company is about to offer us a job, we feel light, relaxed, and optimistic. It's based on the vibe we received and our responses to the questions asked or our tasks. Many of us are serving God and experiencing hardships, which is natural. But, knowing we are doing all we can (our interview tasks) to please Him and maintain a healthy relationship with Him should make us feel like God is about to pour a tsunami of blessings our way we can not receive all by ourselves! It may not come when we want it, but it will always come on time! Knowing that, joy is produced and we can still maneuver with a grateful manner.

CHAPTER 5

EXERCISING PEACE

Think about a time in your life when you worked a hectic schedule. Suppose you had major demands at work you needed to handle abruptly while going through a messy divorce or break up. At the same time, you and your best friend are feuding and all you can say is, "Lord, please get me through this because I need some peace!" We are accustomed to requesting peace when experiencing a plethora of distractions and discomfort, not understanding that we often define peace in terms of what it is not.

Now think about a leaking faucet. This can be problematic when hearing the annoying sounds of water dripping especially after receiving an outstanding water bill. We know we can call on a plumber to fix the problem, but depending on our financial circumstances, we pass the plumber idea and decide to patch the faucet ourselves. After patching it, we say, "Now I can rest in peace." Right? Wrong! Peace is not an absence of distractions, discomfort or conflict. In comparison to joy, we can experience peace in the midst of problems.

Peace is found in the presence of harmony or community. So, how can we find peace through harmony? In the above examples, each situation pertains to ourselves, not others. Without ill intentions, we are so self-serving. Naturally, when we experience problems within our own space, we focus on them alone, creating a discord between others, or we isolate ourselves from the issue at hand to escape the problem. When doing so, we must understand that the problem will not go away, we just prolonged the journey towards fixing it, often allowing the situation to snowball into something bigger than it was before. This applies to our health, our relationships with others, and maintenance within our own selves.

Peace occurs when we surrender to God to be in His control. Through God, we shall find peace. This occurs when we develop a harmonious relationship with God so that He can develop our minds, hearts, and will. We have a hard time surrendering control to a God who created us for many reasons. Either we are not spiritually connected to Him or it is because we live independently daily. Maintaining peace with God will help us establish and maintain peace with others.

He is our source, so let's use Him. We can be so stubborn when it comes to letting go of control. In the previous example I shared about the leaking faucet, this represents what we do all of the time. Instead of calling on the expert, the plumber to fix the problem, we take the most convenient and inexpensive way out. Patching a leaking faucet does not work, so do not do it! The plumber's job is to investigate the cause of the problem, diagnose a solution for it, and then fix it.

We often put Band-Aids on all of our problems and expect it to cure the wound. I would not tell a doctor who wants to operate on my heart to just put a Band-Aid on my chest arguing that the price for open-heart surgery is too high, I cannot endure the pain, and that it would take too much time to heal. As silly as that sounds, this is exactly how we look in the eyes of God. We cry about our health, but don't go to the doctor. We whine about not having enough money, but don't take time to look for a second job. We complain about thieves, but continue to invite them into our homes. When will we learn that when we do less to change the situation, the outcome will remain the same.

So, if we feel like we can't find peace, we probably need to make some changes in our lives, and that starts with letting God do what He is able to do which is deliver. He is our source to calm our minds and ease our hearts. Like each spiritual fruit, it requires work to acquire peace.

PEACHY PEACE

A phrase I often use is, "Everything is peachy keen!" This means all is good. Our mindset play an important role on our overall health. When we speak that everything is all good, we declare it in hopes that everything is indeed okay.

This phrase has nothing to do with peaches, but it reminds me of the fruit itself, being that peach is in the phrase. Peach cobbler is one of my favorite dessert dishes. It simply puts me in a good mood, hence making me feel peachy keen!

Peaches are natural fruit that have many health benefits. Among many, I would like to point out two. The first one is that they help the body maintain a healthy nervous system. The magnesium in peaches help prevent stress and anxiety and help keep us calm. It helps bring our stress levels down so that we can enter a place of relaxation and comfort. I compare peaches to peace, although peaches will not give us peace, the nutrients found in them can put us in an emotional state of calmness.

Second, peaches are known to detoxify the body. They aid in flushing out harmful toxins from the liver and kidneys. Herbal peach flavored detox tea is a known way to detox. Anytime we detox, we are eliminating unhealthy substances from the body and at the same time, we are no longer placing toxins in our body. Toxins are poisons derived from microorganisms that cause harmful diseases to occur. If not treated well, diseases could be detrimental to our health, which causes more stress, pain, and discomfort. When we consume peaches, we decrease the chances for diseases to form.

We receive peace; however, through God. This means in each decision we make, we should allow God to lead us. When we receive peace, we do not escape from our problems. We escape from stress associated with our problems. Stress, negative thoughts, doubt, and fear is detoxed from our minds, allowing us to experience freedom in circumstances that are beyond our control. The purge is needed, but we need God to help us. Anatomically speaking, the adult human body is composed of up to about 60% of water. We can't survive without water for no more than a few days. The same applies to God. Being that He is our creator, without Him, we will never thrive nor will we experience peace in our lives.

Real peace does not just come and go; it is ongoing. It must be rooted and exercised in our hearts and spirit. Many of us are not satisfied because we do not understand what peace is. Because of this, we often send requests for it. Instead of drinking water when we're famished, we opt to drink an entire Coke, which will satisfy our thirst for a short while, but then we find ourselves feeling dehydrated and in need of water later.

If we think about how peace affects us, the more of it we have, the better we can cope with tough situations. Sometimes, problems are unavoidable, so it is important that we are prepared to face them. When we're not prepared, we inadvertently add layers to the problems that currently exist by making kneejerk decisions under pressure.

Peace allows us the ability to make wise and calm decisions, because it is built on the foundation of God's word. Isaiah 53:5 states, "But he was pierced for our transgressions; he was crushed for our iniquities; upon him was the chastisement that brought us peace, and with his wounds we are healed" (NIV). When we think about all of the sacrifices made unto mankind, we shouldn't help but feel safe no matter what we face because God stayed true to His word. Because of God, we are able to produce peace each day. So regardless of our circumstances, with God, everything is peachy keen!

The Story of Elisha

Panic and peace are like oil and water. They just do not mix. If you asked yourself if your panic outweighed your peace, what would you say? Keep it real. Some of our stress levels are so high we are hospitalized due to stress alone. That is such a detriment to our health and God does not want to see us endure that. But, we do it to ourselves more often than we should.

Instead, peace and harmony mix. For instance, in 2 Kings 6:8-23, a prophet of God named Elisha demonstrated what peace looks like in what appeared to be a stressful situation. A Syrian king initiated war against Israel. Elisha was able to tell the King of Israel the conversation that the King of Syria spoke in private. When the King of Syria found out, he was enraged and pursued to capture Elisha immediately.

Eventually, a large Syrian army surrounded the city and Elisha on horses and with weapons. Elisha's servant panicked, trying to figure out what to do. Elisha's response to him was, "Do not fear, for those who are with us are more than those who are with them" (2 Kings 6:16, NKJV). Ironically, Elisha, the person of interest who could possibly be captured by an army of men was calmer than his servant, someone who was not considered to be a person of interest.

This demonstrates an example of enormous faith and peace Elisha had, because by sight, there was no escape. He was practically outnumbered. He could have panicked like his servant and simply thrown in the towel. Interestingly, we can show great strength, courage, and faith when experiencing conflict from a distance. But real strength occurs when it arrives in your back yard.

Elisha had so much peace in his heart and faith in God that despite what was happening around him, he knew he was protected. His simple words were a declaration that no matter how many people are against you, God's power alone is all he needed. God's power is all we need also. We may have entered a season of loss, suffering, rejection, provocation, worry or pain. Let's face it, when it is heavy, that is what we focus on. Holding on to all of the heaviness will force us to focus on it. Once we release the dumbbells of each pain we are toting each day and give them to God, we no longer need to focus on the problem, rather, we persevere through our situation with a joyful attitude and peace in our spirit, knowing that God will grace us through it. Elisha developed peace in his heart, so when he faced this challenge, he was strong enough to exercise it.

As I mentioned earlier, peace is harmonious. Instead of Elisha asking God to just remove the army from his space, he calmly prayed to Him during all of the confusion happening around him and asked God to open the eyes of his *servant* so that *he* could understand. How remarkable!

This is an example of the loving work God can do through us. Elisha was so content, he did not pray for himself, but he prayed God will do a great work in the spirit of his servant. God opened the eyes of the servant, and he began to see from a new set of lens (verse 17). At this time, the army intensified; however, his servant could now see warrior angels standing between Elisha and the army.

Note that problems may intensify before they go away, but if we focus on the problem and not the provider, we too will be frightened and not be able to see God's plan. As the Syrians approached Elisha, he did not run. He did not hide. He merely prayed not asking God to harm them, but instead, he asked God to strike them with blindness, and within moments, the army became blind- not by Elisha's might, but God's power.

Elisha then led the army back to Samaria and when they arrived, he asked God to open their eyes. When the King of Israel saw them, he asked if he shall kill them, but Elisha ordered not to do so. Instead, he told him to provide them with food and water and release them to their master. The Syrian army ate, drank, and returned to their master. Thereafter, the Syrian army never bothered Israel.

There are many great examples of love, faith, peace, joy, kindness, and self-control that came from this story. Our flesh would tell us to solve the problem by capturing the army or killing them. Why? Because this seems like it would put an end to the problem. However, that only creates more anger from the other side, creating an ongoing war.

Has someone tried to provoke you? Did you entertain them? If so, more than likely, they continued. At some point, we must learn to show great character better than we can speak it. How can we ever find peace by engaging in the conflict? It will continue to fester. Elisha taught the Syrian army a great lesson through his generosity and kindness. Going back to Proverbs 25:21-22, when responding according to the will of God, the Lord will reward you, and He indeed rewarded Elisha.

Abram and Lot

The story of Abram and Lot in Genesis 13 also provides an example of how we should walk in peace. Abram and his nephew Lot traveled together both carrying possessions that were too great for the land to support them that they were unable to dwell on it together. Conflict arose among the herdsmen of Abram and Lot over the land regarding how they would co-exist with all of their possessions.

Instead of engaging in the conflict, Abram told Lot he did not want to fight with him, nor did he want their herdsmen to fight among each other, so he proposed that they separate so they could have their own space. He also allowed Lot the opportunity to choose whichever portion of the land he desired, so that he could dwell in the opposite direction. Lot viewed the land before him and noticed that the land of Jordan was the most beautiful and well hydrated land. So he chose to venture towards Jordan. Abram went in the opposite direction to Canaan.

Now, Abram could have claimed the better land because he was his uncle, or forced himself on the land of Jordan, but instead, he had so much peace in his heart that it did not matter to him at all. The peace within him allowed him the ability to calmly assess this situation and diffuse the argument. Because Abram allowed the God in him to outweigh his flesh, God showed favor towards Abram by allowing him to inherit the land of Canaan. Because Lot had a selfish heart, little did he know that the decision he made from his own flesh led him to an area where wicked men dwelled and were sinful against the Lord (Genesis 13:13).

Philippians (4:7) "...and the peace of God, which surpasses all understanding, will guard your hearts and minds through Christ Jesus" (CSB) tells us that we may not understand in the moment, but if we trust in God, He will show us the way. The path of peace will lead us towards many hidden treasures. I am quite sure Abram was not expecting anything in return, but God always rewards those who honor him. Have you heard of the expression, "He may not come when you want Him, but He'll be there right on time?" That is because God is an on time God, and His timing is perfect.

PRODUCING PEACE

It is difficult to get in character of the fruit of the spirit because of the mercy God has on us. We may feel at times that although we made irrational decisions consequence free, or experienced a period of happiness after a wrongdoing, that those decisions were okay. For instance, if we conspired against someone else and got away with it, we may feel that the decision made was for our good because we felt vindicated. Understand that God has mercy on us all, so even when we make wrong decisions, His love for us is undeniable.

To be honest, many of us expect God to give us some passes, hence, mercy. However, if we have gotten away with ungodly behaviors, we may feel that everyone around us has a motive against us. Our conscious convicts us and paranoia and trust issues form.

When life gets real, peace is impossible to acquire when we try to find it from our own might, separate from God. We must learn to let go from our own desires and will and realize who is in charge. The scripture, "Peace be still" (Mark 4:39, ESV) is a reference of Jesus calming the wind from a storm. Jesus proved that during a frightening moment in the midst of a storm on a small ship that His faith was strong. Even His disciples were afraid, but Jesus allowed peace to be the anchor to stay the course and cling to hope.

Again, peace is not acquired when things in our lives are perfect. There are many people who have fame, fortune, and can have any tangible item they desire, but suffer from depression. Many people throughout this world lack many possessions, but have peace in their hearts and minds because their primary focus in on God. Without God, regardless of what we possess, we will find emptiness. With Him, the sky is the limit.

We can't control our circumstances, but we can control how we persevere through them. One way is to set time aside for God by setting an ambiance to invite peace into our lives. Just as the environment is relaxing when visiting a masseuse, set a spiritual ambiance and center yourself in God's presence. Surrender your heart to Him, delve into His word, and connect through prayer.

UNWRAPPING PEACE

Many people may have developed thoughts that in order to obtain peace, we must be free from distractions, busy schedules, and cluttered minds. However, we often experience difficulty in obtaining peace because of lack of faith. In a controlled environment, we can accomplish some of the most difficult and fearful tasks. When we visit amusement parks, we spend money to wait in long lines to ride extravagant and thrilling roller coasters that thrusts us high into the air, whipping us back and forth, up and down, upside down and around tracks. We know that the ride will be bumpy, slightly painful, and filled with unexpected surprises. Because we trust the quality of the amusement park, are pleased with testimonial reviews, and feel safe when strapped to the cart, no matter how rough the ride will be, we trust that we will return to the ground safely, despite of experiencing potential whip lash and queasy stomachs. Therefore, we feel comfortable with the journey.

When things are in our control, we exercise more faith in things we want to pursue. What makes faith difficult is when we release control to God, allowing the desires of the spirit to rise above the flesh. What is puzzling is that although we know that we are protected when God lead us, we still respond in fear, which blocks us from obtaining peace. We must give more credit to God than we do. John 14:27 states, "Peace I leave with you; my peace I give you. I do not give to you as the world gives. Do not let your hearts be troubled and do not be afraid" (NIV). I love how plain this scripture is. Because He does not give to us as the world gives, obtaining peace from the Holy Spirit will feel different from obtaining it from the flesh.

WE EXERCISE PEACE WHEN:

- We can compromise with others to avoid conflicts.
- We have accepted God in our lives and trust in Him.
- We can no longer sweat the small stuff.
- We can put our pride aside and accept constructive criticism.
- We can face adversities without panicking.

- We are no longer focused on what people say about us.
- We learn to harmonize with others.
- We become optimistic.
- We love ourselves and others.
- We stop focusing on our enemies and focus on God.
- We are free from paranoia.

Peace is exercised through a combination of things- through faith, wisdom, patience, humility, compassion, and mercy. God will allow peace to those who trust Him.

CHAPTER 6

EXERCISING PATIENCE (LONGSUFFERING)

My mother used to say, when it rains, it pours. I have felt that many days. Can you imagine facing hardships over and over again? There are people that feel like they cannot catch a break, and it is exhausting! Think about an aspiring athlete who has faced numerous injuries and can no longer participate in the desired sport, or a law student who just can't seem to pass the BAR exam, or how about the single parent who has to work several jobs to catch up on bills only to face new financial duress. Enduring patience is painful at times. Understand that if you have struggled in your season of wait, you are not alone. I experience it and so does many people around us, whether we know about it or not.

SURVIVING A SEASON OF WAIT

Patience is the next fruit of the spirit. The bible refers it to longsuffering because when enduring a season of wait, we may suffer long. Waiting for a breakthrough is one of the most difficult things we experience because we want to see our hard work pay off.

"…but we ourselves, who have the first fruits of the Spirit, groan inwardly as we wait eagerly for adoption as sons, the redemption of our bodies. For in this hope we were saved. Now hope that is seen is not hope. For who hopes for what he sees? But if we hope for what we do not see, we wait for it with patience" (Romans 8:23-25, ESV).

In this season, it is not uncommon that we will become tired. As a matter of fact, some of us will become exhausted as our flesh and spirit wrestle. When I think about being patient, I immediately refer to the movie, *"Cast Away"* starring American Actor, Tom Hanks. *"Cast Away"* is a survival drama that portrays a man, played by Tom Hanks, who was stranded on a deserted island after surviving a major plane crash. All he had to survive were remains from the plane's cargo. This man suffered; however, there were many things to be grateful for. At the height of suffering, we do not always think about the bright side of our situation and neither did he. What was plain to him were the facts before his eyes, which was the mess he was thrown into.

There he was, stranded with minimal food, a shortage of water, a few supplies, no shelter, no civilization, nor means to communicate. To make things worse, he had a fiancé at home whom, after several weeks without hearing from him after learning about his plane crash, assumed he died. What a huge pill to swallow! What would you do in such an uncomfortable situation? You plan to marry the love of your life and in your mind, you believe your companion feels you deserted them. It is so hard to endure patience when things are no longer in your control.

This man did what many of us would do. He tried to survive through his circumstance. Does this sound familiar to you? When we reach difficult times in our lives, we reach survival mode as well. When we feel like our expenses exceed our income and no one will offer that promotion to us, as difficult as it is, we show up to our jobs and try to put on a happy face. When our children take wrong paths in life and we feel like they will never understand the errors of their ways, we still make attempts to counsel them. When people try to tear us down, diminish our worth, and defame our character, we try to hold our heads up and press through the hurt. We have a natural desire to succeed, even in our period of wait and discomfort. What makes things laborious for us mentally, physically, and emotionally are failed attempts to make things better, no matter how hard we try.

That is what happened in *"Cast Away."* Above all this man was going through, he made several attempts to signal for rescue, but failed. He even made a very close attempt to be saved, but failed as well. In his efforts to survive, he endured injuries and pain. Just imagine discovering that in order for rescuers to find him, they would need to search an area as large as the size of Texas times two. At some point, when do you give up and lose hope? Would you give up?

After four long years, he was rescued. Scriptures from Isaiah 40:28-31 reassures us that when we reach a point of exhaustion, we must go to God so that He may replenish us with strength. We understand that God has a plan, and mid-way through it, we get tired.

Many of us are tired because we have been trying to hold our heads up after being beaten and attacked by the enemy in so many ways that we reach a point of exhaustion. It's one thing to struggle without being bothered, but imagine struggling while under constant attack AND while trying to exercise God-like character through His spiritual fruit. So when people provoke us, we're trying to remain humble. When bosses on our jobs mistreat us, we do our best to exercise self-control. When family members can't get their lives together, we try to exercise goodness, and when we do not feel love is reciprocated to us in return, we try to exercise love. All of this happens while we engage in our daily tasks even when we become ill. If we dig for strength through our own might when we experience fatigue, it is the biggest mistake we could ever make.

We seek advice from family and friends all while knowing God has all answers, but unfortunately, we go to him last. We must understand that when we are tired, we do not think clearly, nor do we behave in the best character. Imagine trying to function on 48 hours without any rest. Would we represent our best self? Would we be able to focus? All we would be able to focus on is what our bodies need, which is sleep.

So, instead of exerting energy in the right places, the body begins to do all it can to produce energy to keep us awake. As a result, we either make poor decisions because we did not properly assess the situation, or we simply crash.

God is aware that we will need to recharge. All of our capabilities comes from Him. Just as a car needs fuel from it's owner when it runs out of gas, we must go to our creator when we need replenishment. Isaiah 40:29 states, "He gives power to the weak, and to those who have no might He increases strength" (NKJV). Isaiah 40:31 assures us, "but those who wait on the LORD shall renew their strength; they shall mount up with wings like eagles, they shall run and not be weary, they shall walk and not faint" (NKJV).

Job

The story of Job portrays an example of what patience and faith looks like in the sight of God. Job was a God-fearing man who dwelled in the land of Uz. He was a very wealthy man who had a wife and ten children. Satan knew Job loved God, but he wanted to prove to God that if he could strip Job of everything he owned, his demeanor towards God and faith in Him would change. God allowed Satan to destroy everything Job owned including his crops, servants, livestock, and to make things worse, a terrible storm blew down his son's house and killed him and all of Job's children. When Job heard of all of his losses, he shaved his head, dropped to his knees and worshipped God saying, "…Naked came I out of my mother's womb, and naked shall I return thither: the LORD gave, and the LORD hath taken away; blessed be the name of the LORD" (Job 1:21, KJV).

Think about this. Many of us would be beyond devastated. Imagine a hurricane rushing through destroying all you owned including your children. The first of many questions we would ask is, "Why is this happening to me?" According to the bible, instead of panicking, Job never sinned nor blamed God. He worshipped him! Many of us can not name a single person we know who would respond the same way.

One day things are great and within seconds, almost everything is lost, including your children, all unexpectantly! How insane is this?

Job had feelings like any other man. He dreaded the day this may happen to him because he understood that God gives and God takes away. In the years Job acquired wealth, he maintained a close relationship with God. Many people grow further away from God when they acquire success. They may worship and praise God in the beginning, but as God continues to bless them with opportunities and things, they feel they no longer need God, then inadvertently rely on their own strength. Job had already exercised a great appreciation for God by remaining humble and wise. So when devastation occurred, although extremely hurt, he worked harder to remain true to God. Romans (12:12) states, "rejoice in hope, be patient in tribulation, be constant in prayer" (ESV). Before Job fell to his knees and worshipped God, he grieved, but he did not blame Him. He worshipped Him.

The devil was not finished with his attempt to destroy Job in hopes that he would curse God. In Job 2, the devil smote Job's body with sore boils from his head to his toes. At this point, Job's wife questioned his integrity and God. What was happening before her eyes was too much for the both of them to bear, and she thought of blaming God. However, Job, although physically ill, remained strong in his faith by believing that God would deliver them.

Job's friends came over to provide comfort, probably wondering what Job did to deserve this punishment. It is not uncommon that when we experience hardships in life that people around us judge us by assuming we did something wrong. It can be difficult from an emotional standpoint, because not only are we suffering physically and mentally from the actual mess, we also think about the opinion of others and stirred rumors. Patience generates humility, and Job was humble by remaining true to God, and not himself. He did not make excuses to save his reputation, nor did his character change.

We must also take into account that Job still had emotions. He may not have cursed God in the beginning, but he did curse his own existence in Job 3. He felt so much pain he was not at ease, and his heart was troubled. The devil tried to take him down physically so that his mind could become weak. In this experience, Job learned that when you bite the hand that feeds you, you would be chastened. 2 Peter 3:9 states, "The Lord is not slow to fulfill His promise as some count slowness, but is patient toward you, not wishing that any should perish, but that all should reach repentance" (ESV). Many times, we are chastised with more wait when we blame God for our troubles. Even after we blame Him foolishly, we still cry out to Him and expect Him to deliver us.

Job felt the pain from all angles. I'm sure he felt the frustration from his wife. The devil's attempt to hurt him was successful. He knew God had a plan and was willing to accept it, but it is hard to do so when you are emotionally, physically, and mentally drained. Job had to be patient that God would deliver him, and later, God restored Job with a double portion of what he had in the beginning.

PATIENCE AND DISCIPLINE

The fruit I compare patience to is a coconut. As a child, I would hear adults say that stubborn people have heads as hard as coconuts, because it takes a long time to get through their stubbornness! In many cases, that is how we are. When God says, "No," we try to force situations to occur only to realize we prolong our blessings. Coconuts are referred to as seeds, nuts, and a distinct form of fruit, They have a hard outer coat that is layered with shells leading to a white sweet meat that can be used in multiple ways, along with milky sweet water used for drinking. I compare coconuts to patience, because if we are really hungry, in search of food, and a coconut is all we could find, like in *"Cast Away,"* we will need to be patient when trying to crack it open.

When we want or need something in life, we too, become hungry for it, and make several attempts to make a breakthrough. But when God says, "Not now," how should we respond?

Hebrews 12:7-11 reference how to endure hardships as a form of discipline. Just as we discipline our children, God chastises us. Discipline helps us learn from mistakes so that we do not repeat them. Some of you may think, "God, I haven't done anything wrong," and you may wonder why you are enduring a waiting process. We must also take into account that God is preparing us for His purpose, just like in the story of Job. He ordained a path for us to walk on, but we typically develop our own plans without seeking His approval through prayer.

Suppose your young adult daughter decides to go on a road trip for the first time with her girlfriends for the weekend. You know her friends and trust they will conduct themselves in a mature manner. You caution your child to take the Interstate because it is faster and a more familiar and safe route, but she decides to take back streets because she wanted to view the scenery, without informing her father, nor even asking him if her plan was a wise decision. Midway through her route, she discovers they had to close the road down due to a hazardous spill. Way to go GPS. Now, her only option is to turn around and head back towards the Interstate.

She realizes she is in need of gas and her next available station is about ten miles away. She did not listen to her father's instructions; however, if needed, she knows that if her car ran out of gas, she has no choice but to go to him to ask for help. In the eyes of any parent, we may feel the decision she made to take unfamiliar routes to a place she desired to go, but never been to, made no sense. However, we do the very same thing. Although in the example, the man's daughter did not necessarily do anything wrong, nor did she have bad intentions or motives, but because she did not follow the plan her father put in place, her trip was delayed.

We experience those moments as well. God tells us to go right, but we get distracted within our own thoughts and decide to venture left. We may even have stellar plans, but we rarely ask God for approval and guidance regarding each decision we make in our journeys. Instead, we seek advice from the opinions of friends and family. If any of you lack wisdom, ask God, who generously gives to all without finding reproach, and it will be given you (James 1:5, NIV). Remember, God is a way-maker and a provider. Only He has the answers that would lead us down the path He ordained. We must ask with faith, believing that God is able and is willing to help us.

According to Isaiah 43:16, "Thus says the Lord, Who makes a way through the sea and a path through the mighty waters…" (NASB), we must learn to love and trust Him enough to lead us to our destinations regardless of what we see or think. Only He can lead us to His promises.

Joseph

Joseph's life is an example of how to be patient through trials as well (Genesis 37-42). Joseph was the son of Jacob who took care of sheep and goats with his brothers. His father, whom designed a special robe just for Joseph, loved Joseph more than his brothers. His brothers felt his father favored him, so they despised him.

One day, Joseph brought Jacob a bad report about his brothers. Joseph also had dreams he would tell his father about. He had different dreams where he saw himself reigning over his brothers. When he mentioned it to them, they hated him even more. Thereafter, Joseph told his brothers of another dream he had about the sun, moon, and stars bowing down to him (Genesis 37:9). His brothers became more envious of him, so they plotted to kill him. However, they were persuaded to not harm Joseph, but to hide him in a cistern in the wilderness. They stripped Joseph of his robe and threw him in the empty cistern without water nor food, and left him there to die.

They later decided that killing Joseph would offer them no gain, so they sold him as a slave to Potiphar, an Egyptian officer, for twenty shekels of silver (approximately eight ounces of silver). To cover their wrongdoing, they slaughtered a goat, dipped Joseph's robe in the blood, and claimed to their father that Joseph was devoured from a ferocious animal. At this point, Joseph did not understand what was going on and why. He could not understand how his brothers of the same father would do this to him. However, throughout this experience Genesis 39:2 ensures that God was with Joseph and He allowed Joseph to succeed in everything he did even as a servant in the home of Potiphar.

Although Joseph encountered a very unfair situation where he was betrayed by his family, almost killed, and then sold as a slave, he still worked very hard. Potiphar saw that the Lord was with Joseph, allowing him favor and success in all he did. Therefore, he promoted him to be in charge of his entire household and property, and because of this God blessed the entire household.

Just when things began to run smoothly, Potiphar's wife began to lust after Joseph. Joseph refused on numerous occasions to engage in an affair with her. This angered her to the level where she made false accusations against him, claiming Joseph tried to rape her. When Potiphar heard of this, he sent Joseph to prison. In this story, it seems that each time Joseph took a few steps forward, he was taken back several leaps. The bible points out that he was an extremely hard working man, as many of us are.

We may have faced moments in our own lives where we felt the very same way. Imagine finally paying off a long-term debt, and then get robbed of your entire savings. In all Joseph experienced thus far, it was behind the jealousy and envious ways of others who maliciously and intentionally tried to harm him. Understand that no matter what we go through, we must believe that God is there to help us along the way.

At this point Joseph is in jail, and Genesis (39:21-23) informs us that the Lord was still with Joseph because he was faithful in the Lord. Joseph faithfully waited and trusted God in this process whole-heartedly because it showed through his actions. God made Joseph the favorite prison warden, where he later was promoted to be in charge of all other prisoners. Even in prison, Joseph succeeded! When we feel we are in our period of wait, although we may feel like we are imprisoned, everything is still, and God is silent, God wants us to know that we are not burdened. It may feel that way because we are not moving at the pace we would want to and the place we are in is very unpleasant, but God wants us to exercise patience and trust Him in the process, because like in Joseph's situation, God paved the way through Joseph.

Joseph continued to remain obedient to God and was later appointed ruler of the entire land of Egypt. The entire time, God had a plan. Joseph was part of it, but was unsure about how it would be executed. He was taken on a roller coaster ride of ups and downs, but through it all, God found favor in him. He was betrayed and sold into slavery, but Potiphar found favor in him through God. He was imprisoned, but the wardens found favor in him through God. In Joseph's journey at each trial, he exercised patience. He was not a perfect man who just accepted everything that came to him. I'm sure he missed his father, hated working as a slave, and felt lonely in prison, but he worked in excellence through discomfort and wait. Galatians 6:9 states, "And let us not grow weary of doing good, for in due season we will reap, if we do not give up" (ESV). Patience was needed to allow God to do a great work through him.

No matter what we experience in life, we must continue to strive even when we cannot see the results we desire within the timeframe we want to see it in. One of the things I love about coconuts is that they are multi-purpose fruit that are rich in vitamins, minerals, and have great health effects. The oil it produces is great for maintaining healthy skin, nails, and hair. The lauric acid found within coconuts lowers bad cholesterol levels and keeps arteries healthy. At the center of the coconut the liquid endosperm, known as coconut water. Coconut water is a healthy replenishing drink as well as a metabolism booster. Just like in *"Cast Away"*, when in need of food, the coconut can replenish our bodies; but in order to get the center, we must endure patience through work and perseverance, because it won't crack open by itself. When we get to a point when we can exercise patience like Joseph, we too, will be able to enjoy all that God promised us.

UNWRAPPING PATIENCE

As I shared with you before, I am also learning to exercise patience. In Chapter 1, I revealed that our thoughts and our faith in God determine what decisions we will make in life. There is an expression that states, "Where there is a will, there is a way." Along the way is a period of longsuffering. I learned how to exercise patience when I least expected it.

As I stated in the introduction, I endured a tough time in my life. When my son was four years old, I was nearing an end of a two-year custody battle for him. My son and I were briefly without a home for about two months, living in hotels for a few weeks, and at my friend's home for a few more weeks. I found a way to exit a relationship that was not ordained by the will of God, and I accepted that wholeheartedly.

Many women and men are afraid to make decisions for many reasons. They are either unsure of how they will take care of themselves financially, are afraid to simply be that single parent, are afraid of a messy divorce or custody battle, or are even afraid to be on their own. Realistically, I believe many enter relationships not expecting the worse to come from it. Some people are more concerned about what others will think of them. In all instances, fear is of the unknown, because we do not know what the future holds by leaving. At some point, I had to come to realization that this relationship was not based on the will of God. We were unwed. I was open to accepting that it was not for me and have faith that God would forgive me and see us through it.

Although things became stressful, financially draining, and mentally exhausting, I knew that the choice I made for us was not poor. It is often that when we are faced with trouble after we made a tough decision that we second-guess or even place blame on ourselves. There was no time nor energy for me to throw a pity party. In this, I had to find strength, self-reflect, and trust in God.

Many of us struggle with making decisions. We waver thinking that because the decision(s) we made did not lead to a quick and desirable ending, that the decision was wrong. James 1:6 states, "But let him ask in faith, with no doubting, for the one who doubts is like a wave of the sea that is driven and tossed by the wind" (ESV). I too, thought those things, not realizing that everyone goes through different journeys and sometimes, it just takes a wealth of time to reach our destination. I am learning that it really took more time for *me* to strengthen my character of patience.

WE EXERCISE PATIENCE WHEN:

- We are able to trust the process while enduring the process.
- We submit to the will of God.

- We can still thrive and work hard in this season.
- We dismiss doubt and invite hope.
- When we no longer focus on the duration, we focus on building our relationship with God.
- We can be productive during the waiting season.
- We are able to pray and give thanks through the process.
- We are able to exercise restraint from our flesh while allowing God to use us.
- We are able to live by the will of God.
- We are able to relinquish control.
- Our focus is no longer in the past.

CHAPTER 7

EXERCISING KINDNESS

I grew up in a small community among many neighbors who were like family. Everyone knew each other and many parents tried their best to make sure children in the community were safe. We rode the bus to and from school, and I remember rare instances when our parents worked late shifts, one of my neighbors would usher us into her home once we were released from the bus at our bus stop after school. Her name was Mrs. Thomas. Mrs. Thomas, as well as a few other people, was a great neighbor and a good friend to my mom. She was usually available anytime we needed supervision. She understood the need and she did not mind. Her direct care towards us was so loving. She did not have the fanciest home or much entertainment, but one thing I always remembered was she would offer us an after school snack. She did not have to, but she did it anyway, and I loved it! Mrs. Thomas was famous for her homemade teacakes, and I was such a fan of them. She would bake them and sell them in the community and on days when we would visit after school, she would offer them to us. She would also help us get started with homework and allow us time to play outside. All that she did for us was because she was thoughtful and kind.

As I got older, I unfortunately did not see many communities such as the one I grew up in. Everyone seems to be so focused on themselves and their own situations, they do not have time nor make time for others. Think about it, whether you live in an apartment complex or a house, how many of you know the neighbors around you or have actual relationships with them? If not, isn't it funny how we can aspire to live in beautiful homes in nice neighborhoods with great amenities, zoned to the best schools, with frequent police patrol, but are strangers to our own neighbors?

I remember just friendly gestures among my childhood neighbors as we drove down the streets, everyone waved. If someone was stranded, within minutes, someone was there to offer assistance, and remember, we did not have cell phones at that time. It was a small community of support and care that helped many residents establish relationships with each other and feel safe. I do not see that much today.

ARE WE KIND?

Think about the last time you encountered someone in need. Did you help them out? It may have been the homeless person tapping on your windshield asking you for money at a stoplight, or the girl scouts selling cookies at a local supermarket, or firefighters on street corners asking for fundraiser donations. It could have even been the single parent trying to get through a public door with her hands tied trying to hold on to a baby stroller with her crying baby in her other hand. Was she offered any help? Did we roll our eyes at the homeless in judgement? Did we turn our heads when the firefighters approached us? And did we ignore the girl scouts once they approached us?

At some point, we have become de-sensitized to people's feelings and needs. Philippians 2:3-4 states, "Let nothing be done through selfish ambition or conceit, but in lowliness of mind let each esteem others better than himself. Let each of you look out not only for his own interests, but also for the interests of others" (NKJV). With so many violent acts we hear about on news occurring in broad daylight, it's a shame that selfishness, hatred or even lack of wise counsel has made many people feel they must walk around guarded at all times.

Mannerisms have become less regarded by many people, thanks to many television programs, music, and social media outlets. It's no wonder why we see rare forms of chivalry from men to women when we live in a society where it is perceived as cool to degrade women and inflict harm on each other. We also see women and men fighting on television insulting and attacking each other's wealth or lack thereof. We see teenagers and adults who instead of breaking up fights, gather around and record barbaric torture. Children are drawing guns on their arms mimicking tattoos from their favorite celebrity, thinking guns are the way to resolve conflict. Bullying has become a climbing issue in so many forms where even children have taken their own lives behind the demeaning tongues and abusive hands of their peers. Adults have lost respect for their children and self-control as they verbally attack each other or fight in front of their children.

As the world practice this behavior over and over, people eventually respond to what they see even within their own households. Continuous cycles of finding love in all of the wrong places, hurt and anger from losses, illnesses, or financial duress, and violence can all lead us towards feeling like we are on an emotional roller coaster. If we can not show love and kindness towards our own families, it's hard to exemplify those traits towards others.

KINDNESS HEALS

According to Galatians 5:22-23, kindness is the fifth listed spiritual fruit. God wants us to exercise kindness by developing a mindset of being thoughtful and considerate to others. Hebrews 10:24-25 shows us that acts of kindness will encourage others to respond the same way. "And let us consider how to stir up one another to love and good works, not neglecting to meet together, as is the habit of some, but encouraging one another, and all the more as you see the Day drawing near" (ESV). Since kindness is a fruit of the spirit, when comparing kindness to an actual fruit, I compare it to pineapples, which is another favorite fruit of mine. Pineapples are sweet tropical fruit that have several great qualities, but two main qualities they have are that they alleviate common colds and heal wounds.

If you think about it, kindness can make bad things go away and heal as well. Have you ever had a bad morning? For those of you like myself who are not "morning people" think about a morning that was not the best. Let's say you had a presentation to present at work that morning and you needed to get there early to set everything up. You got up early, pressed your way to discover you are stuck in traffic without an available exit around. At this point, you're annoyed because things are not happening as planned. You finally get to work, late, and frustrated at the fact that you have so much to do in practically no time. Low and behold, a co-worker helps you quickly get prepared for your presentation. Their kind helping hand helped alleviate the developing problem and was able to put you at ease. Kindness makes us feel comfortable with others so that we can function on one accord.

So how can kindness heal wounds? We've all probably felt wounded before. Suppose you discovered your spouse was cheating on you and you are about to go ballistic! You decided to contact your best friend to tell him or her about what happened and how you plan to seek revenge. Your friend listened to you vent, then explained how that revenge was not the best idea. Instead, your friend offered to pick you up and take you out to steer your mind away from the pain. You had a great time, but during that visit, your friend also expressed how you should best handle the situation and offered to help you along the healing process. This act of kindness involves love, because the friend in the scenario was looking out for the best interest of you. Good friends don't tell us what we want to hear and motivate us to do wrong. They respect us and lead us towards making decisions for the better.

Proverbs 31:26 states, "She speaks with wisdom, and faithful instruction is on her tongue" (NIV). Kindness is showing consideration towards others without expecting something back in return. Kindness, like love, does not discriminate. In the aforementioned scenario, although we may feel that seeking revenge is needed, God designed us to show kindness to people we may or may not know even when we feel people do not deserve it.

Boaz and Ruth

Kindness goes a long way. The story of Boaz and Ruth, (Ruth 1-4), is an example of how kindness affects others. Boaz was a wealthy and powerful man who showed compassion and loving-kindness towards Ruth, a foreign Moabite widow. He was not only humble and merciful towards Ruth, but he showed brotherly kindness towards his servants each day. Because he was a kind master, he had faithful and dependable servants, causing a harmonious community.

Exercising kindness does not always mean that everyone we are kind to will receive it in a good way. Some people are drowning in their own misfortunes at times that even kind gestures do not move them. In this story, I can only imagine there may have been some people who felt that way, but it was clear that Boaz was consistent in his character enough to create a trusting and amicable environment, even when he experienced bad days. When Boaz greeted his workers, he would say, "The Lord be with you!" and his workers responded the same way (Ruth 2:4, NIV). They also cared enough about each other that they expressed their kindness by praying for each other.

Ruth's mother-in-law, Naomi suffered the loss of her husband and her two sons. During her time of struggle and grief, Ruth and her sister-in-law decided to be with Naomi to provide her with comfort and support. When things in their home town of Moab began to improve, Naomi insisted that her daughters-in-law move back to their hometown and find new husbands so they would not have to live alone (Ruth:1-9). Ruth's sister-in-law did so; however, Ruth stayed with Naomi, sacrificing the opportunity to move back to a better land, and journeyed to Bethlehem with Naomi.

One day, Boaz noticed Ruth, a stranger working extremely hard in his grain field. When Boaz noticed her, he inquired about her. Boaz found out that Ruth, a converted Gentile widowed woman decided to work to sustain herself and her mother-in-law. At that point, he treated her well. He provided her with plenty of water, roasted grain, and an abundance of barley he allowed her to gather to take back to her mother-in-law. Ruth was curious to know why Boaz was so kind to her. It's interesting how we can feel like in order for someone to be kind to us, we had to have done something previously to earn it. Ruth never knew this man, but saw he showed favor towards her and wondered why. In Ruth 2:11-12, Boaz explained to her how noble it was of her to move to a land with people she did not know to care for her mother-in-law after her husband's death. He also told her, "May the Lord repay you for what you have done…" (Ruth 2:12, NIV).

This example shows how God allowed the time in Ruth's life when she took loving care of her mother-in-law to establish Ruth's reputation as an honorable believer in God. At that time, I can assume that Ruth was not compassionate towards Naomi for a personal gain. She sacrificed her own opportunity to move back to her native land to, instead stay to help Naomi during a time when she felt all hope was gone. When Naomi felt like God has turned His hand against her (Ruth 1:13), Ruth stayed to assure her that she was loved and cared for. Ruth may have encountered frustrating moments as well, but she stayed committed to doing good for others. Thessalonians 3:13 reminds us of this: "As for you, brothers, do not grow weary in doing good" (ESV).

This story also shows how Boaz took the opportunity to exhibit God-like character through kindness. Boaz could have been selfish, disregarded Ruth, not open up his home to her nor provide her with access to his surplus. Some of us have developed a mentality that we worked too hard for what we have, so what we acquire is ours. Don't get me wrong, many of us work hard and are still struggling, so I understand. However, being judgmental will always prevent us from obtaining God's spiritual fruit. Matthew 7:1-2 states, "Do not judge, or you too will be judged. For in the same way you judge others, you will be judged, and with the measure you use, it will be measured to you" (NIV). If we put ourselves in the shoes of others, how many people would we expect to pass us up before we were offered their help? In many instances, little things go a long way. Both Ruth and Boaz were humble in character and thoughtful through their actions without seeking anything back in return.

The Good Samaritan

The Parable of the Good Samaritan always come to my mind when I think about acts of kindness. In this parable (Luke 10:25-37), Jesus described a man who was attacked by robbers. They stole his clothing and beat him severely, leaving him for dead. What is interesting about this story is that although this man was hurt, beaten and stripped of his clothing down a main road in the city, a priest and another citizen who passed on the same road never stopped to rescue the man. Can you recall a time when you were stranded and no one stopped to help you, or even when you were the onlooker who never stopped to service someone else? In this situation, would you stop? I understand if you feel like you could potentially be put into danger, but does that mean to not provide assistance by calling 9-1-1 from your cell phone? Many people shy away from helping others because they do not want to get involved. But if you were in need, would you appreciate someone else's involvement?

Jesus mentioned that a Samaritan who was traveling came over and not only rescued the man, but provided loving care to him. He bandaged his wounds, loaded him on his donkey, brought him to an inn, and did not just drop him off, but paid for his shelter and continued to take care of the hurt man. Jesus described him as a neighbor because he had mercy on the robbed man. He did not know him, but felt compassion for him during his suffering.

God wants us to have the same heart towards not just people we know, but to all human kind. This man took time away from his travels to assist someone in need, and many of us have a hard time doing simple things such as opening doors for others or helping elderly people load groceries into their cars. In Romans 12:10, we are reminded to, "Be devoted to one another in brotherly love; give preference to one another in honor…" (NASB). We should not feel that we can only help others when things in our own lives are where we want them to be. In doing that, conditions are placed on why and how often we help people. Remember, kindness is showing compassion to others regardless of our current emotional, financial, and health state. It is less about us, and more about others.

BENEFITS OF KINDNESS

As I mentioned earlier, the consumption of pineapples can help heal wounds. The bromelain within the fruit helps the human body heal itself properly. Compassion on others through kindness can also heal wounds. Sometimes, nice gestures towards people can provide them with the attention they need for the day. Some people only receive insults, demands and harsh judgements consistently and feel imprisoned in their abusive environment. Interestingly, it is not always easy to identify people who experience this because they mask it or are too afraid to mention it to someone. A simple compliment or a nice greeting could be a statement that encourages others to think of themselves in a more valuable light. Many people are naturally uncomfortable with expressing themselves or problems they face. We could just be the light they need in their darkness at any given time.

I remember I was on a flight to Phoenix, AZ to attend a residency. I was tired from my work week and mentally exhausted at the thought of what I was about to experience in my six day class. At that time, all I wanted was a restful flight, but of course, the passenger next to me was a talker. He was very friendly and I was in return, but all I could think of was, "Didn't he realize my eyes were closed when he began to speak to me?" In hindsight, it is quite humorous because when we experience moments like this when we just need our alone time or quiet space, instead of listening to others and considering their needs, we expect them to consider ours. However, I engaged in a conversation and learned a lot about him.

Within the last three months, he lost his mother, wife, and sister. He was traveling to attend another funeral, his uncle, and began to reminisce about all of the individuals in his life who recently passed. It was obvious to me that he needed someone to talk to, because not only did he have a lot to say, but he found joy in the conversation with a total stranger, me. All I was able to offer was my time, but it seems it was more valuable than anything else was. Colossians 3:12 states, "So as those who have been chosen of God, holy and beloved, put on a heart of compassion, kindness, humility, gentleness and patience..." (NASB).

He did not know me, and I did not know him, but in that conversation, we exchanged stories and encouraged each other. I thought what I needed was rest, but it was proven that I needed the conversation as well.

Kindness is offered as a shield of protection. It can prevent people from seriously harming themselves. Although the world is filled with tools and people we can access, many people feel quite lonely within it. Things will not provide us with peace and joy. God's anointing and the loving kindness from people helps us live in unison rather than just exist.

According to the Centers for Disease Control (CDC), in the United States alone, suicide was a leading cause of death in 2016 (National Institute of Mental Health, 2018). Although many factors contributed to this, regardless, it is still suicide. Peace, joy, love, and faith in God would not cause anyone to destroy their own God-given life. 1 Timothy 6:6-12 describes how we only gain in life when we find contentment by being in God's presence. Suicide occurs when we feel all hope is gone, all contentment is lost, we have reached darkness, and lost a strong connection from God.

God uses us as vessels to encourage each other and spread the word of God to each other. Ephesians 2:10 reminds us, "For we are His workmanship, created in Christ Jesus for good works, which God prepared beforehand, that we should walk in them" (ESV). Offering help to those who appear to be bothered can help people open up to us as a cry out for help. Essentially, yes, there may be moments in our lives when we encounter hardships or when people abuse us to the core. If and when we reach that point in our lives, we may rely on others to help us during those trying times and talk us off the ledge.

Jesus' Kindness

Jesus practiced numerous acts of kindness throughout his life on Earth. He went above and beyond to help people through His teachings, His healing, His helping, and His sharing. Jesus' actions were healing. He was moved with compassion, not with the mindset that He had to, but it was rooted in His heart to treat others with great care. He actually entered each person's situation and became involved in their suffering. Talk about putting himself in their shoes! And He continued to do this.

Here is an example of how Jesus considered others. Jesus has been traveling with His disciples and healing many people. Soon after John the Baptist, a well-known God-fearing preacher who even baptized Jesus was beheaded (Matthew 14), Jesus decided to depart to a deserted place to be alone. When crowds of people from the city found out where Jesus was, they followed Him like sheep following a shepherd. When Jesus saw them, instead of getting upset or feeling bothered, He was moved with compassion for them and continued to heal their illnesses and loved ones.

Later that evening, Jesus' disciples came and told Jesus He should send the crowd back home to buy themselves food. Jesus could have gladly sent them back to their city so that He could be alone. Instead, He provided them with something to eat. At that moment, he took only five loaves of bread and two fish, blessed it, and was able to feed over 5,000 people abundantly with it. Kindness is authentic generosity produced from our spirits towards people we know, do not know, deserve, or do not deserve it. His planned moment of alone time turned out to be a Jesus hosted party of over 5,000 people!

Have you ever felt down or needed to get work done and just wanted some alone time, but your phone rings or you receive that knock on your door from a friend who just needed to vent? Although you have needs of your own, you are also aware that they need you as well. Imagine you knocking on Jesus' door needing to talk to Him after finding out someone so dear to him died and He not only attended to your needs, but cooked an entire meal for you as well. That's just how unselfish He was.

WHAT KINDNESS IS AND WHAT KINDNESS IS NOT

Many people get kindness confused with being nice; therefore, kindness is underrated. A nice person would ask, "Are you hungry?" A kind person, such as Jesus would provide food for the hungry without even asking. It's about going the extra mile to support someone in need, not just being polite. A nice person may compliment others, but a kind person will offer wise counsel. A nice person does not have to care about what others may go through, but a kind person cares the same way the person in need does.

We must understand that sometimes direct attention goes a long way, even if it is just to listen to someone speak, extend a little comfort, praying for someone, or texting them a heartfelt affirmation to let them know we are thinking of them. Romans 15:2 states, "Let each of us please his neighbor for his good, to build him up" (ESV). It's not about providing people with tangible things, because let's be honest, many of us do not have them. It can be frustrating at times to only have a little bit of money, then experience someone tap on our windshield to ask us for it, or when our time is limited, it seems more people are in need of it. Sometimes, we can only give what we have, whether it's time or money, but when we provide it in a loving way, it's received in a big manner. Kindness is exercised when we have loving and compassionate hearts. What I love most is that Jesus did not even know these people and He treated them all fairly.

We can show acts of kindness authentically in several ways because there are many opportunities to be kind each day and we must take advantage of them. If we notice someone is alone and feeling isolated, attempting to speak to them and make them feel welcomed may help make them feel wanted. If someone is being mistreated at work or school, words of kindness and wisdom may help brighten their day. If someone looks lost and needs assistance, stepping in to help point them in the right direction may be appreciated.

Kindness does not discriminate. We can offer acts of kindness to children, elderly, bosses, employees, and to those who are disrespectful, angry, and stubborn because love and mercy are attributes of kindness. Ephesians 4:32 states: "Let all bitterness, anger and wrath, shouting and slander be removed from you, along with all malice. And be kind to one another, tenderhearted, forgiving one another, even as God in Christ forgave you" (CSB).

The toughest part about being kind is being kind to people who are bitter, complainers, unappreciative, and difficult to get along with. Some people may ask for something and receive it with an expectation that they deserve to have it, without offering thanks. Remember, everyone did not grow up learning about manners, and if they did, they may not always use them. Our kindness should not stop on the account of how others respond to us. Kindness is not a sign of weakness, but it shows great character and strength.

My father was a kind and loving man. I speak of him because as a female, a strong and loving father figure was important to me. In addition, everyone I encountered has always said great things about him. My father was a man who was not perfect, but showed his tender heart. He was always strong in my eyes and I developed a healthy fear of him through respect and love. I definitely never wanted to disappoint him. He was a "Jack" of all trades- literally. He experienced many great successes and was always a helper in the community.

My father reached a point in his life when he endured a lot of disappointments and devastations. Within just a decade, he was laid off from his job of over twenty years, experienced the demise of his marriage, suffered the loss of both of his parents and his close brother, and entered financial stress. It seemed all he worked hard for was ruined and he had to start all over. I witnessed him hustle jobs and acquire new trades. I saw the frustrated moments and the tears. Through all of that, my father helped his siblings in need by either offering them a place to live, offering financial support during his time of struggle, or hire people to work with him on construction projects as he worked hard to establish a business for himself. Although he experienced problems and pain, he always supported others through theirs. He was always in attendance and showed condolences to friends and family whom lost loved ones, and he was very reliable.

One of the things I cherish most about my father was our conversations. No matter what, he always set aside time to listen to me vent, express my ideas to him, and tell the funniest jokes. Psalms 119:76 states, "May your unfailing love be my comfort, according to your promise to your servant" (NIV). His love for me was unconditional.

What I can truthfully say was that my father was not just a listening ear, but he was honest with me and decisions I made or wanted to make and he always referenced God. Don't get me wrong, he was a father to me, not a friend and there were boundaries, but we had a comfortable relationship with each other. When he needed to chew me out, he did through love. Then he would point out the error of my ways, and then teach me right from wrong. He was a gem in my eyes, because there were moments when my father and I faced hardships together, and no matter what, he always considered my feelings and his entire family ahead of his own. I would never ask for anything, but if he felt I needed something, he would send it. He was simply kind. It wasn't about what he did for me. It was about the love he showed through what he did for me. His actions towards myself, my son, my family and others made me want to reciprocate it back to him and most importantly, be more like him.

UNWRAPPING KINDNESS

Kindness is a sweet fruit of the spirit, but no matter how sweet it is, the flesh wants to fight against it. In our fast-paced, time-consuming, everyday tasks, our flesh tells us that we do not have time to help someone, listen to their needs, or that it's not our problem. We must reach a point in our lives when we no longer make excuses.

We make excuses habitually anytime things in our lives get too tough. I am quite sure people on drug or alcohol addictions struggle in their journey towards sobriety, and when the going gets tough, the excuses come. How often do we think to ourselves that we would rather not work with a new hire because they will slow us down? So, instead of helping them, we avoided them. When was the last time we had to break a promise because we were too busy or too tired to fulfill it? The excuses come especially when forgiving an enemy. We know we should forgive them, but hesitation rises.

I will admit that it could feel quite awkward at times to exercise kindness. Our spirit is a willing vessel (Matthew 26:41), but our flesh fights it through fear and or pride. In all of the examples I have highlighted thus far, God was able to carry out greater testimonies of His power we carry through the spirit. Kindness is a type of character that spreads light to others in the attempt to help them experience love and regard each other's feelings. Allow kindness to cure the common cold of hatred, disgust, selfishness, and violence for kindness is a trait that can be learned best when seen.

Be wise when kind unto others. If being kind causes grief, then it's not God's will. For instance, we often feel good about doing kind deeds, such as giving money to others when in need or being the "yes" person when people ask us to render our services, time, or ideas. Those temporary feelings ware off when we find ourselves stressed out afterwards. If we are burdened through generous acts, they are not genuine. We often respond through temporary emotions, then become disappointed and regret the kind deeds we did for others or hold resentment towards those we were kind to. We should not force kindness. It must be applied obediently through the will of God and with an open heart.

WE EXERCISE KINDNESS WHEN:

- We are able to be generous to people even when they do not deserve it.
- We are able to be generous to people even if they do not appreciate it in return.
- We aim to motivate those who need a boost.
- We willingly make provisions for those less fortunate.
- Our actions show we are team players.
- We relinquish the "crab in the bucket" syndrome. We uplift others so we can all make it to the top together.
- We help others without a motive.
- We can rescue someone from an uncomfortable/ unsafe situation.
- We provide friendly advice.
- We teach people how to do something without judging them.
- We become the shoulder others can lean on.

- We can apologize for our wrongdoing.
- We can take ownership in being a better example of ourselves.

In all we do, we must remember those who were also kind unto us and allow the cycle to continue onto others.

CHAPTER 8

EXERCISING GOODNESS

When you hear the word, "good", what do you think of? If someone asked you what goodness meant to you, how would you define it? I asked myself this same question and actually struggled with an answer. When I took time to think about it, I realized that I acknowledged that something was good when it met or exceeded my expectation. For instance, I may say the food at the restaurant I visited was good. It satisfied my need and it did not disappoint me. I may also feel that the waiter's service or the band's performance was good. In these examples, my interpretation or standard for what is good to me may be different for different purposes. No matter what, when someone refers to something as good, it is a benefit to someone.

Goodness is the next fruit of the spirit. Like kindness, good deeds benefit people in some way. Whether we have a good friend, a good spouse, a good mentor, or a good provider, goodness is beneficial, and when exercised properly, it is helpful to us holistically.

You may be thinking that something that is good to one person may not be considered to be good for someone else. For example, a thief may successfully rob a bank and think that because he or she got away with it, it was a good act. Although their benefit was new wealth, it was at the expense of others, which is not good. An individual can beat someone up and although he or she won, it caused harm to the victim. A competitive co-worker can sabotage a colleague to maintain the highest sales record, but again, their behavior prevented success and potential growth for the colleague. So, my theory of how I viewed goodness was not entirely correct. We may find that we may make wrongful choices without penalty for a short while, because of God's love and mercy on us. However, it only works in our favor temporarily.

Goodness encompasses the act of being truthful, righteous, just, and forgiving. When we practice goodness, it is not necessarily for our own good, but for the good of others. I remember when I was younger, I would witness more people take accountability for their actions. If a person accidentally scratched a car next to them in the parking lot because they opened their door too wide, they would actually write their contact information on a note, point out the damage, and place it on the windshield of the car they hit.

Now, it's nearly impossible for supermarkets to take responsibility when shopping carts their customers use cause damage to vehicles in their parking lot. Individuals with credible knowledge of accidents or abuse that occurred now flee scenes because they simply do not want to get involved. The scriptures tells us to, "…not be overcome by evil, but overcome evil with good" (Romans 12:21, NIV). A "hit and run" mentality along with expecting people to take responsibility for other's wrong doing completely disregards people's feelings concerning things they work hard for and their environmental state.

UNDERSTANDING GOODNESS

Many people have heard of the, "An apple a day keeps the doctor away" expression. This implies that apples have good benefits that keeps us healthy. I compare the spiritual fruit of goodness to the fruit, apples, because apples have many great health benefits. They reduce stroke risks, lowers levels of bad cholesterol, improves brain health, and reduces diabetes risks. All of these benefits provide us with elements that are helpful for our bodies. According to I Corinthians (3:16), our bodies are our temple, and God's spirit dwells in us. Therefore, we must exercise goodness according to how God envisioned us to.

Being good to others benefit us in several ways. Goodness is virtue and holiness towards one another. A person of goodness character is one who has high moral standards, filled with the spirit, and desires to be a blessing to others. You may be wondering what this looks like. Well, anything truthful is goodness. We live in a society where many people would do anything to sell a product, even lie about it. Commercial advertisements on television display products to appear to be good for us, but after we buy in to them, we soon realize the quality of the product does not match the price. Telemarketers and many sales representatives may find ways to lure consumers in to buying products by guaranteeing them they will receive discounts, but they later find out there are several conditions surrounding the advertised discount. New technological products, such as game systems, cell phones, or other devices are advertised about every two years offering a few different features for a ridiculous amount of money, only to break just in time for a newer and more expensive product to surface the market. Because many consumers want to "keep up with the Jones'", it is easy to be taken advantage of. Goodness is the opposite of that. It is not gaining at the expense of others. It is about living in truth through every action we take. James 4:8 reveals, "Cleanse your hands, you sinners; and purify your hearts, you double-minded..." (NASB). Essentially, this scripture tells us we should purify our attitudes and stop straddling the fence between God and the world. It is easy to get sucked into doing what is convenient, comfortable, or even pressured by our peers. However, doing good is always about being honest, and listening to the angel instead of the devil on our shoulders.

Anything righteous is also a form of goodness. Righteousness refers to doing what is morally upright and of virtue. Kindness, forgiveness, honesty, fairness, and love are all characteristics that describes righteous behaviors.

> "If a man is righteous and does what is just and right—
> if he does not eat upon the mountains or lift up his
> eyes to the idols of the house of Israel, does not defile
> his neighbor's wife or approach a woman in her time

of menstrual impurity, does not oppress anyone, but restores to the debtor his pledge, commits no robbery, gives his bread to the hungry and covers the naked with a garment, does not lend at interest or take any profit, withholds his hand from injustice, executes true justice between man and man, walks in my statutes, and keeps my rules by acting faithfully—he is righteous; he shall surely live, declares the Lord God" (Ezekiel 18:5-9, ESV).

According to this scripture, a righteous person does what is right, not do what is wrong then persuade others and themselves that their wrongdoing is right. A righteous person lives through the will of God. A righteous person does not put others down, but is kind enough to help them during times of trouble. A righteous person does not scam and steal from others, but gives instead. A righteous person does not cheat the law for his or her own personal gain, but makes fair and truthful decisions. A righteous person walks by faith in God and not by the sight of man. A person of righteousness has self-control and is able to resist the flesh and trust the spirit to lead them.

Goodness does not always feel good. We often behave in a way that leads us to believe that. For instance, the consumption of alcohol may make us feel good temporarily, but soon after it wears off, the feeling goes away. Instead, too much of it could cause us to actually feel bad. Eating junk food daily may make us feel good, because sometimes, food makes us happy. But an unhealthy diet can cause us to feel bad about our new formed appearance and detrimental health state. Premarital sex appears to be the norm in our society because sex sells and is accepted. It may be a good feeling to engage in it, and it may seem to be right, because "everyone else is doing it", but again, it only seems to be good until we feel empty inside after hearts are broken, diseases are discovered, or we come to our senses that it is a sin.

On the other hand, vegetables are an example of things that are good and beneficial to us, but may not be something we enjoy. Doctor and dental visits are good health practices, but fear of needles and potential drilling may prevent people from visiting. Reading the fine print before signing any contract is wise and beneficial to the signer, but many people skip that process because it may be inconvenient to read at that moment. Sometimes, what feels good and convenient is not good, and what is good does not always feel good nor convenient. Just like exercising love, joy, peace, patience and kindness, developing the character of goodness is not easy and will take time to acquire.

When I think about goodness, I refer to the, "What would Jesus do?" question. Before retaliating against someone, ask yourself, "What would Jesus do?" Before looking down on others in judgement, ask yourself, "What would Jesus do?" Before you justify your wrongdoing, ask yourself, "What would Jesus do?" Before you mislead someone or lie to them, ask yourself, "What would Jesus do?" Matthew 12:35 states, "The good person out of his good treasure brings forth good, and the evil person out of his evil treasure brings forth evil" (ESV). As I mentioned in Chapter 1, *Exercising Your Mind,* whatever you deposit into your mind will represent what you release through your actions. According to Romans 7:18-19, goodness is not something that is easily acquired and it is definitely not something we can generate from our flesh. It, like all other spiritual fruit takes time to plant, nurture, and grow.

Washing of Jesus' Feet

In Luke (7:36-50), Jesus taught a great lesson to one of the Pharisees at his home. A sinful woman approached Jesus at the table with an alabaster flask of fragrant oil and stood at His feet crying. She felt remorseful of her sins at the presence of a sinless man. She cried so hard, her tears began to flood at Jesus' feet. She then used her tears to wash Jesus' feet, her hair to wipe them dry, and then anointed His feet with the fragrant oil. The Pharisee commented under his breath in judgement saying, "This Man, if He were a prophet, would know who and what manner of woman this is who is touching Him, for she is a sinner" (Luke 7:39, NKJV). Jesus heard him and responded to him by referring to an example of debtors.

He told the Pharisee that a creditor had two people who owed him money. One debtor owed him five hundred denarii and the other debtor owed him only fifty denarii. The creditor forgave both debtors when he learned they were both unable to repay him. Jesus asked the Pharisee which debtor would forgive the creditor more, the one who owed him more or less? The Pharisee stated possibly the one whom was forgiven more. At this moment, Jesus proved His point and elaborated. He explained that the debt, or in our cases the weight of our sins does not matter. Goodness, like love and kindness has no conditions. The creditor placed no conditions on the debtors, because no matter how much they owed individually, they were both in need. However, the debtor who owed five hundred denarii probably forgave Jesus more because he received fair treatment although he had a larger debt.

We live in a world filled with judgement. We as sinners are quick to judge someone for their sins as though as if we are perfect. We may all reach points in or lives when we may experience debt, cause harm in our relationships, or make desperate decisions that we may be convicted for later. We can not walk around looking down on people who had a past or have a present worse than our very own today. Walking in goodness means we should have forgiving hearts, for we would only hope someone would forgive us during our time of need.

Jesus told the Pharisee how the woman of many sins entered his house and treated Jesus with kindness as if He was in her own home. Her heart was so sincere that He trusted her in her remorse for what she did in the past. She did not have water, so she used tears to wash His feet, probably her best oil to anoint Him, and she kissed His feet repetitively. What I love about this parable is that no matter what we did in our past, we can still exercise goodness and be forgiven.

If you have reached a point in your life when you feel convicted of things you have done in the past that you may not be proud of, understand that you can still be used by God. 1 John 1:9 affirms, "If we confess our sins, he is faithful and just to forgive us our sins and to cleanse us from all unrighteousness" (KJV). Because the woman loved so much and was honest in her actions, Jesus forgave her sins, regardless of how many they were because love keeps no record of wrong. Jesus's goodness was shown through love, for He stated, "...to whom little is forgiven, the same loveth little" (Luke 7:47, ASV). The less we forgive, the less we love and exercise goodness. The more we forgive, the more we show goodness through love. As a result, the open heart and good deed of the woman was reciprocated from Jesus when He allowed the woman's sins to be washed away.

God's Goodness

As I mentioned earlier in the chapter, goodness is fair and just. Unfortunately, though I frequently see reports of people abusing their authority and using their intelligence for their own good and not for the better interest of others. I have seen judges, politicians, and bosses get sucked into forming groups such as parties or cliques, composed of people they cater to and defend regardless if they are right or wrong. Have you ever experienced someone at work who received a promotion you questioned? This person is an obvious friend of the boss and although intelligent, is unprofessional and rude. You may have witnessed that person disrespect customers and when a complaint was filed, the boss covered it up. Unfair, right? During campaign season, you may have seen politicians display a caring and loving character in the public, but once sworn in office, they do not fulfill promises and make unethical decisions.

The older I got, the more I began to experience how little people care about others. Sometimes, we do not pay direct attention to these behaviors until we experience the bad side of it ourselves. As I stated in Chapter 6, *"Exercising Patience,"* when my son was two years old, I walked into an ugly custody battle. At that time, I did not know what to expect, but as a defendant, I fought hard for primary joint custody of my son all while trying to re-establish myself as a single parent again.

I learned quickly how abusively unfair the court system can be. Unfortunately, some people learn not to do good, but use their knowledge as leverage to deceive. For someone like myself who was new to this game of charades, it seemed quite apparent to me that any attorney and judge who acquired years of experience in family law would see through any masquerade of acts. I had knowledge of my child and his wellbeing along with any legal documentation I needed to win this case. I most importantly, maintained my integrity and honesty throughout the trial and duration of the case. When particular attorneys and the judge maintained a solid relationship, the ugly side of "politics" became real through bias, deception, and lack of actual concern for the well-being of our child. After two years of having primary joint custody of my son under temporary orders and through a frivolous trial, the judge reversed the ruling, listing me as the non-custodial parent in a joint conservatorship.

I never received a reason why this occurred until after I received my appeal ruling. My intuition led me to believe that it was based on an inside job. All I could do was ask, "How could a working mother with no record of violence, drugs, theft or anything lose primary custody of her only child?" I knew at that moment that I was in a unique situation where God was trying to intervene, but of course, I did not understand God's purpose for my life at that time because things did not appear to be fair.

Everything surrounding the ruling was so bad. Anyone who knows me know that my son and I are inseparable, so losing access to him during the majority of his weekday was very difficult to handle. You may be wondering, "What does this have to do with goodness?" Well, when we exemplify characters other than goodness, for instance, becoming self-serving, deceitful, untrustworthy or unethical, we could definitely cause damage to people who experience weak moments. Those traits can be the straw that break the camel's back and could be discouraging and a trigger that lead people to retaliate in ungodly ways. This is not what God intended and He is not pleased to see us deviate from His plan, because we were established for His purpose through His sacrificial love. Ephesians 2:10 states, "For we are his workmanship, created in Christ Jesus for good works, which God prepared beforehand, that we should walk in them (NKJV). Anything that is not done through the will of God, is not good.

At that point in my life, I will admit, I was devastated. I definitely felt that God let me down. I was at a point in my life when I thought I would win the case and that it would be put to rest, but God had other plans for my life. It was a big pill to swallow, and just when I thought I calmed down, more questions came! I wondered, "How could you allow unfairness to prevail? How could I feel in my spirit victory, and be let down like this? Don't you want what is best for my child?" And here are the infamous questions, "Why am I going through this? What did I do to deserve this?" How will we get through this? Those thoughts entered my mind and I found myself getting angry each time they came to me. I knew not to allow the enemy to see me sweat nor mischaracterize myself and God by making knee-jerk decisions, but fighting vindication was tough.

As I mentally tried to prepare myself to withstand a journey to appeal this case, I became a prayer warrior over my child. More than anything, I prayed that he would be safe, that he would inherit a strong moral compass, would develop in a healthy manner, would excel academically, and not feel hurt or pain behind this situation. I had to learn how to continue to be good to my son even from a distance. It's a shame that when some parents feud over child custody, parents retaliate by making each other their focus. They become blind in their fit of selfishness and anger that the central focus, the child is no longer the actual point of concern to them. Regardless of who would receive credit for my son's accomplishments, I still go above and beyond to ensure he is well taken care of spiritually, emotionally, physically, and mentally, because it's not about the parents. All credit is given unto God. James 1:22 reminds us to, "Be doers of the word, and not hearers only, deceiving yourselves" (ESV). It's one thing to know the word, but another thing to ignore it through our actions. Regardless of how painful things may seem, God's grace is sufficient enough for us to still exercise goodness.

LESSONS LEARNED

I later learned that God allowed this to happen to me to prove to me just how real He is. This may sound so bizarre to you, so let me explain. Psalms 119:68 references the Lord by stating, "You are good, and what you do is good; teach me your decrees" (NIV). We often focus on the bad things that happen to us in life as mere punishment and we go out of our way to figure out why it happened, but from sources of no substance nor credibility. God allows things to occur in our lives whether we created that space or not to get our attention. I am by far not happy to have endured this type of pain, but I am grateful for the fact that God loves me so much, He planned a special assignment just for me. He could have overlooked me, like we do others, He could have given up on me, like we do to others, and He could have just let me live life not truly drawn to Him. However, His plans for me (which I cannot specifically see) are so great that He took time to teach me through a difficult trial. He is the epitome of goodness.

I compare this type of goodness to a coach who takes time to train an athlete who sees so much potential in him that others do not see. He challenges the athlete more than others through extra practice time, lectures about the sport, and by matching him up with opponents who appear to be stronger, quicker, and more seasoned than he is. The athlete may not understand why the coach is so tough on him, but because he wants to grow, and since the coach is credible, the athlete listens, trains harder, and learns.

The coach in this example exercises goodness towards the athlete, because everything he does for the athlete is with benevolence and in high regard. No matter what state we are in our lives, and no matter what appears before us, goodness is around us always through God's divine presence. Only He could provide us with an abundance of strength to help us ignite goodness within our own hearts. Forgiving wrongdoers is a struggle for many, including myself. However, not through our own might, but through the power of God will we acquire the good fruit.

UNWRAPPING GOODNESS

The Parable of the Sower

It was revealed in Genesis 1, that God was pleased with His creation of the heavens and the Earth. Because of it, He saw that at each phase,

His work was good. God referenced His good work at least seven times in the first chapter of Genesis, because it met His expectations. If we think about this, we often do the same thing. When producing something we envisioned for the first time, such as painting a canvas, writing a song, or starting a business, at each successful phase, we become proud of our accomplishments. God did the same thing and found that His work was good. The book of Genesis also states that God created us in His own image (Genesis 1:27). Therefore, it is important we live according to His expectations, His purpose, and His plan. If we established a business, we would expect individuals we employ to work under our expectations as well.

In Luke 8, Jesus spoke about the Parable of the Sower. He mentioned that seeds, or the word of God, can only be planted on good soil. In the parable, the sower planted seeds in different locations. Those who received it on rocky ground received it with joy when they heard it, but because they had no root, it could not grow when they were tested by God. Those who received it among thorns became chocked by life's worries and pleasures, allowing them to not mature. Those who received it on good soil retained it, because they had a good heart, were noble, and listened to the word of God with an abundance of faith and hope.

There are good people in this world. Are you one of them? Good ground produces good fruit, and a good house stands on a good foundation. God is trying to plant the seeds of all of His spiritual fruit within us, including goodness; however, we must be planted on good soil to allow it to take root. When the heart is pure, hears the word of God and obediently responds, goodness is exercised; and God's expectation is fulfilled.

WE EXERCISE GOODNESS WHEN:

- We are able to not make decisions at the expense of others.
- We are slow to judge and quick to forgive.
- We are merciful unto others.
- We instill hope and wisdom in others.

- We are able to show goodness to others and not look to seek credit or gratification.
- Our behaviors are genuine and from the heart. We do not seek praise from others.
- We make ethical and morally correct decisions.
- People trust our motives.
- We treat all people fairly.

CHAPTER 9

EXERCISING FAITH

A scripture I heard throughout my entire life is from Luke 17:6, "…If you have faith as small as a mustard seed, you can say to this mulberry tree, 'Be uprooted and planted in the sea,' and it will obey you (NIV). For a while, I did not understand how only a little faith could help us move mountains. My reason for not understanding was that I, at that time, never grasped the concept of what faith truly was.

Faith is divine belief and trust in something we can not see. Many of us struggle to exercise faith when we reach moments in our lives when things are no longer in our control. Because we are used to figuring things out through logic or according to how things appear to us, it is difficult to trust that God will literally make a way out of no way. As I discuss faith, you will realize that it encompass all of the spiritual fruit I listed before, such as love, joy, peace and patience. If you can exercise those characteristics, then trusting God would not be as difficult, especially through tough circumstances and during a season of wait.

It is not easy to remember God's presence and believe in His power when we face circumstances that are difficult and uncertain to us. We speak from our lips how much we believe in God and that we have faith in Him, but actions speak louder than words. For instance, have you ever strived to lose weight and struggled to see results? Your fitness instructor reassured you that the inches and pounds would melt off as long as you stuck to the routine, but frustration settled in because you have invested time, energy, and money towards your exercise regimen and dreadful diet, all to not see any results. Especially when in comparison to others on the same regimen, you began to see changes in their bodies and you thought, "I'm glad for him or her, but when will I see my results?"

In the weight loss process, efforts towards achieving your goal of losing pounds or inches will also be at the expense of humility and patience. In some weeks, you may have experienced weight loss, and in other weeks, you may have remained stagnant. There may have also been moments when you have gained a pound or two. It could be due to muscle mass or water weight; however, those who were successful in their weight loss journeys were aware of the possible bumps they may have stumbled on along the way, made adjustments, and recommitted to their goal. Your fitness instructor, the expert, had faith that the longer you exercised and remained consistent in your regimen, you would be able to see the results you expect. They have also helped others meet their goal.

This example reminds me of how we respond when God tries to instruct us on how to handle circumstances we face all of the time. God sees and knows beyond what we could ever imagine because He ordained a path for us to walk on. The moment things become difficult and we enter circumstances that are beyond our control, doubt enters and we waiver in faith. Hebrews 11:1 states, "Now faith is confidence in what we hope for and assurance about what we do not see" (NIV). We must be careful not to lose faith in the process nor feel discouraged if we do not see results even after weeks of discomfort and sacrifice.

Jesus

Many times, God will place us in periods of extended delay even as we aim to exercise faith. It's almost like we are running a marathon that will not end! Trust me when I say that I have a lifelong testimony regarding delay! Doubt and fear could lead us to slowing down in the race when we become disobedient with God. For instance, Jesus is a perfect example of someone who exercised faith as He continued His race. Although Jesus knew that He would be mocked, tortured, insulted and killed (Luke 18:31-34) because His death was God's plan, on the day of His crucifixion, I could only imagine the pain Jesus endured physically, mentally, and spiritually.

Jesus knew He had a purpose to fulfill and that it would please God, so He knew He had to endure it. This man was betrayed, imprisoned, whipped, violently beaten, spat on, mocked and insulted, all while wearing a crown of thorns that were twisted on His head, and while bearing a heavy cross through the city. If any of us were in that position or even witnessed a loved one or friend in that position, we would allow confusion, fear and pain to settle in and question God's love for us. Many of us would quit because what we see before our own eyes is not what we hoped for. As a matter of fact, the hardships we prepared to face are even more difficult for us to tackle alone. My point is that God has a unique way of showing us that we are not strong enough to handle things without His divine power. Guards pierced Jesus with stakes and hung Him high on a cross to die an agonizing death. This was not a quick crucifixion for the bible mentioned that He endured pain for several hours. Jesus kept His faith in God throughout His entire journey, but moments before He took His last breath, Jesus cried out, "Eli, Eli, lema sabachthani?" (which means "My God, my God, why have you forsaken me?") (Matthew 27:46, NKJV).

It is interesting to know that even Jesus questioned God in a time of pain. Not only was He in great physical pain, but could you imagine *how* He felt emotionally? We could all probably relate to a time in our own lives when someone promised us something and after waiting for it with expectancy, they let us down. Maybe it was a long-term boyfriend who promised he would propose to you, but never had the desire to take the relationship to the next level. More than anything, although you were led on, you were probably more hurt emotionally than anything. Now think about a time when you trusted in God with an expectancy to shift some things in your life. You had a vision, deposited time and energy, had highs and lows, experienced your season of delay, and through all of that, you now find yourself with your back against the wall because things have become out of your control and all you can do is trust God. Moses spoke these words to the people of Israel, "Be strong and of good courage, do not fear nor be afraid of them; for the LORD your God, He is the One who goes with you. He will not leave you nor forsake you" (Deuteronomy 31:6, NKJV). Jesus may have felt abandoned after everything He worked hard towards and exercised through love. At this point, all He could physically see was hatred from the citizens; however, God still fulfilled His promise through Jesus' resurrection.

We must learn how to take the passenger seat in this process and let go. It is hard to no longer take the lead, but to follow when we have assigned ourselves as the designated driver for so long. God is saying that He will never leave us nor forsake us, but in order to believe Him, we must develop a relationship with Him and trust and depend on him daily. Faith is like a muscle that must be exercised to develop. My faith last year may have gotten me through some big challenges, but if I do not take time to exercise it beyond that point, it may not be as strong as I need it to be in this year.

David and Goliath

The story of David and Goliath is another great representation of faith exercised at its best. In Chapter 3, *Exercising Love*, I referenced the story of Saul and David. David, from Bethlehem, had brothers who were with Saul fighting against the Philistines. David traveled back and forth from Saul in Judah to tend to his father's sheep in Bethlehem. As he traveled, his father asked him to check on his brothers each visit and David obeyed. Meanwhile, a champion named Goliath came out of the Philistine camp (1 Samuel 17:4-7). He was about nine and one half feet tall, fully armored in bronze, with a bronze javelin, a spear shaft, and a shield.

Not only was Goliath a strong man of great size and fully armored, his declarations to fight terrified Saul and the Israelites. In 1 Samuel

(17:8-10), Goliath shouted a proposal out to the Israelites that if they chose a man of their choice to fight against him and kill him, then the Philistines will be the subjects of the Israelites and serve them. What a bold thing to say! In this moment, Goliath reminds me of what Satan does to manipulate us to make it appear there is no hope. From what the Israelites could see with their own eyes, Goliath was unstoppable and that there was no man that could beat him. They also feared him alongside of all of the Philistines who were fighting against them.

At this point, both armies were drawing their lines facing each other. David ran to the battle lines to check on his brothers. As he spoke to them, Goliath stepped out from his lines shouting defiance against Israel causing the Israelites to flee from him in great fear. It is interesting to know that these men initially went out to battle with energy and encouragement, prior to ever meeting Goliath. Each time they saw Goliath, they lost sight of their goal, and focused on what they saw before their eyes. James 1:3 says, For you know that the testing of your faith produces steadfastness (ESV). It is often that we say we trust and believe that God will carry us through tough times, but when our backs appear to be against the wall, we allow fear to settle in, and quickly lose faith. This is what happened to the Israelites and David saw this.

1 Samuel 17:32 states, "David said to Saul, 'Let no one lose heart on account of this Philistine; your servant will go and fight him'" (NIV). David also stated in verse 37, "The LORD who rescued me from the paw of the lion and the paw of the bear will rescue me from the hand of this Philistine" (NIV). What I love about David's responses is that he remembered what God has delivered him from in the past. It is so quickly that we forget what God has done for us, especially in the height of trouble. Although he was about to enter an unequal fight with a giant who has been fighting since a young boy, his faith in God was greater. Luke 18:27 states, "… 'What is impossible with men is possible with God'" (NIV). What seemed to be impossible, God was willing to make possible.

After Saul saw David had courage, he gave David his blessing to fight and armor to wear; however, David was not used to the armor, so he took them off. Instead, he grabbed a staff, five stones, a sling, and an abundance of courage and faith to approach the army. Let's pause here. Many of us feel as though as if we must have things in order to accomplish things. "If only I had this, I would…" is a statement many of us have thought of. It's okay to be prepared, but let's get real. We will never reach a point in our lives when things are perfect before we can say, "Okay, God I have faith in you." It just do not work like that because, first, God loves to turn situations that appear to be hopeless into deliverance. He does this to remind us that through His might alone, according to our faith, He will turn things around in His miraculous ways. Secondly, God wants us to produce God-like character. We will never produce it with silver spoons in our mouths, so if we encounter moments like David, God is testing our faith in Him. The only armor we need is the full armor of God, which is comprised of characters of God's spiritual fruit, including faith.

As David approached Goliath, Goliath saw what David brought to fight and felt insulted. He became enraged, and began to curse and threaten him death. In this moment, David said, "You come against me with sword and spear and javelin, but I come against you in the name of the Lord Almighty, the God of the armies of Israel, whom you have defied" (1 Samuel 17:45, NIV). David's faith in God allowed him courage and strength to defeat Goliath by slinging a stone into his forehead, killing him. Sometimes, defeating the enemy can cause great courage from us spiritually and little effort physically.

When we wrestle against the spirit, we become weak and tired. Imagine wrestling the spirit with the flesh and then turning around to wrestle the enemy physically. We often repeat this cycle and then wonder why we grow weary and tired. Try to allow the spirit to lead you. It may feel difficult emotionally at times, but it may not require much physical strength. It requires letting go of weight we pick up (control) along with the weight the enemy tries to throw at us (baggage). I can assume that the Israelites felt that the only way to defeat Goliath would be through an enduring physical tussle, and no one wanted any part in that. David was able to defeat a giant, unharmed, through faith in God.

Moses

The book of Exodus paints a great story about how faith can be exercised when we feel like we experience more problems in our season of wait. The chapter begins by introducing a new king of Egypt who feared there were too many Israelites on their land. One of his greatest fears was that if a war began, the Israelites, who were numerous would join their enemies and fight against the Egyptians. Therefore, he devised a plan to mistreat the Israelites by working them in harsh conditions, oppressing them through slavery and killing Hebrew males by throwing them into the Nile River to drown. Just to clarify, the Israelites, Hebrews and Jews were all descendants of Abraham, Isaac, and Jacob. God remembered His covenant with them in which He promised they would be fruitful and multiply, so when His people were mistreated, He looked after them and was concerned.

Moses was born at the time the king made attempts to kill all Hebrew males, but he was rescued and hidden. God saw favor in Moses and appeared to him several years later in Exodus 3:7-10 telling Moses His commands to have him rescue the Israelites out of Egypt. Notice I mentioned that God saw favor in Moses, but at the same time commanded Moses to do something he felt was too big for himself to handle. How many of you are in that position now? Many of us are, and have not come to realization that God is positioning us to push us towards His promise, either because of how big the assignment is, or because we have yet to grasp God's vision for our lives.

In Exodus 3:11, Moses showed signs of apprehension by responding to God, "Who am I that I should go to Pharaoh and bring the Israelites out of Egypt?" At this point, Moses was assigned a great task that he may have felt he was not qualified to handle, nor even willing to conquer. God responded to him by making several commands and promises unto Moses and the Israelites and Moses was still apprehensive. Moses was a man who was not the best speaker, nor was he a popular man. God reassured him protection from His divine lips, showed His power before Moses, and provided him with ways to show people how real God was; however, Moses was still apprehensive.

God offers us signs more often than we think. He answers our prayers in more ways than we can fathom. The problem many of us have is that we do not have faith in God's plan for our lives, but rather try to force our own plans into fruition, not quite realizing that we are exercising belief in our own self-approving works, not the works of God. This happens especially when we enter desperate circumstances when control is removed from us. Instead of asking our guide, God, for answers, we find control in other ways. God was teaching Moses that faith is exercised through obedience. In Exodus 3, although Moses was fearful of the assignment, God reassured several times that He would be with Moses and help him along the way. Throughout the book of Exodus, God gives Moses instructions and Moses questions many of them. Through obedience was he able to see how powerful God was and believe in Him more.

God told Moses that he would make the Pharaoh's heart hard and that his hatred would cause stubbornness and more anger. I can only imagine what thoughts entered Moses' head at that point. This scenario is almost compared to God telling us to stand up to a bully who is mistreating other students or even a boss who is not treating workers fairly. We may be afraid of them as well, and to make matters worse, God is telling us upfront that he will harden their hearts. What an uncomfortable place of pressure to be in thinking that they may also retaliate against us as well. This may have not made sense to Moses at the time, but God had a plan.

God sent plagues on Pharaoh's livestock, a plague of boils on his people and animals, a plague of hail over all of the crops and animals, a plague of locusts and darkness throughout the land, and a plague to kill all of the first born sons of Egypt, all in the attempt to make Pharaoh release the Israelites. In the attempt to make the damages cease, Pharaoh decided he endured enough torture and finally decided he would release the Israelites. In his heart, though, he still did not fear the Lord. After they left, greed and anger set in the heart of the Pharaoh, and they left with their best chariots, strongest troops, and officers to approach the Israelites, who were camped out by the Red Sea.

After hundreds of years of slavery, the Israelites were finally free, for in their eyes, appeared to be a short timeframe. They saw Pharaoh's troops closing in on them and dreaded the fact that they are once again under attack by the enemy, now sandwiched between the sea and their wrath, and it seemed as if the only way for them to live was under their mercy. Sometimes, God will place us in what appears to be a dead end or even a lose-lose situation. The Israelites were terrified! What they were able to see before their eyes was either death or slavery. As a matter of fact, they let their fears be known in Exodus 14:11-12 by stating,

> "Was it because there were no graves in Egypt that you brought us to the desert to die? What have you done to us by bringing us out of Egypt? Didn't we say to you in Egypt, 'Leave us alone; let us serve the Egyptians'? It would have been better for us to serve the Egyptians than to die in the desert!" (NIV)

How many of you have felt that way? We trusted a process, but the moment we saw a difficult situation, we questioned it. Let's think about the victims from Hurricane Katrina. Hurricane Katrina affected many people from New Orleans, Louisiana in August 2005. They lost their homes, relatives, and other assets. Several victims at that time relocated to Beaumont, Texas, only to discover that one month later, Hurricane Rita made landfall, affecting some of the same people. Thereafter, many of the same victims relocated further west to Houston, Texas. One could only imagine how devastating it could be to "start all over". However, since then, Houstonians have endured major flooding and another major Hurricane (Harvey) in 2017. I can only imagine the frustration from those, yet affected again. Just like the Israelites, those from New Orleans may view their journey as one that was not necessary. They may be wondering, "Why was I relocated to Houston to struggle when I could have just struggled at home?" My point is, when it seems all hope is gone, especially when we endure a season of difficulty and wait with expectancy, it is hard to look at a situation that appears to be a dead end with the same hope and faith we once had.

Doubt poured into the minds of the Israelites. Many wavered thinking it may be best to go back with the Egyptians and live the rest of their lives as slaves. Have you ever made wrong turns in life? You took a leap of faith all to discover that when God actually tested your faith, you retreated to doing the same thing? Many times, we live in bondage because our mental state is there. It is not always the external factors that place us there, it is our lack of faith in God. 1 Corinthians 2:5 states, "That your faith might not rest in the wisdom of men but in the power of God" (RSVA). Moses reassured to his people that they would see deliverance if they stood still. Sometimes, standing still is all we are left to do. It is a bittersweet position to be in. However, the sweet part of faith is deliverance.

God did what appeared to be unimaginable. According to Exodus 14:21, as Moses stretched his hand out over the sea, God divided the waters, creating a dry path for Moses and the Israelites to walk through next to the tall wall of water on their left and right sides. As the Israelites crossed the Red Sea, Pharaoh and his army charged after them. As they crossed, God caused great confusion to spread among them, stalling their journey across the sea. Once all of the Israelites successfully crossed, God commanded Moses to stretch out his hand over the sea. Moses obeyed, and God caused the water to flow back down in its place, drowning the entire Egyptian army. "In all circumstances take up the shield of faith, with which you can extinguish all the flaming darts of the evil one…" (Ephesians 6:16, ESV). God provided a solution, fulfilled dreams, and followed through on His promise. Without faith, obedience, courage and expectancy, deliverance would have not occurred.

FROM MISTAKES TO FAITH

Deliverance occurs when we cooperate with God's plans for our life. We must trust that God will not lead us in the wrong direction. When we are able to see God's mysterious plans, it is often that we panic. Many of us respond as though as if He is not qualified enough to lead us in the right path. We know He is real, but our actions show we do not believe in our hearts He is real. Therefore, faith is not exercised. If I decided to take a road trip to a place I desire to travel to, but have never visited before, I would feel more comfortable with allowing a navigation system to guide me rather than relying on my own knowledge. It makes more sense to rely on a source that specializes in leading people in the right direction. Ironically, many of our actions are the complete opposite. Instead, we rely on what appears to be logically right rather than trust in God, our creator and designer of the paths each of us should take in our journeys.

Proverbs 3:5-6 states, "Trust in the Lord with all your heart and lean not on your own understanding; in all your ways submit to Him and He will make your paths straight" (NIV). Without faith, we find ourselves making wrong turns and repeating cycles, prolonging our journeys towards deliverance.

I never knew how hard it was for me to exercise faith until I lost my custody case. At that moment, God handed me a lengthy test, and things began to get real. I've worn this tough exterior my entire life. Many of my family and friends expect me at times to be able to handle tough situations because I've always been so independent. When I lost that battle, I realized I had a limited amount of time to make a big decision about whether or not to appeal my case. The key is that each move I made had to be built on faith and not be based on what someone else expected me to do nor based on someone else's expectations for my future.

Although devastated and knocked down like the boxer in the ring, I not only felt that the judge made an unfair decision, I also knew it. Some people would have given up knowing the ruling was wrong to avoid the headache, expenses, time, and effort they would have to invest in to move forward. I refused to doubt my effort towards seeking justice. I did not agree with the judge's ruling, and had I conceded, I would have made a wrongful decision to not trust God in this process. Above all, God has the final say. We can no longer hold ourselves hostage to man and their authority. Had I remained down, depressed, anguished, and settled in my pain, I knew I would miss very important deadlines and any doors God was prepared to open for me.

Many of us lose sight of our vision quickly when it only develops as an idea. As I mentioned in Chapter 1, *Exercising Your Mind*, we must set expectations to accomplish that dream so that when the enemy tries to knock us down we do not lose sight of it because it is that important to us. Our plan to accomplish that dream should be intentional. Imagine being abandoned in a desert, without water nor food for several days. Your body is deprived, you are beginning to believe that no one will rescue you, and all you have been functioning on is your desire for water. However, you know that water will not just appear. You must work for it and through the will of God. James 2:26 states that "...the body without the spirit is dead, so faith without works is dead also" (NIV). The more miles you put in, the closer you will get to the water you desire. But with God, you will be led to an entire body of water! So, no matter how bad my situation was, I knew that by staying down after taking such a hard hit, I would not be able to move forward if I was not functioning through faith.

Making decisions is not always easy, especially when placed in a desperate situation, because of fear of the unknown. Fear led me to the mistakes of allowing my flesh to lead instead of the Holy Spirit. When making any type of decision we must make our plans known unto God, and make wise investments such as our time, our emotions, our finances, and let go of our pride. Whatever it is, with faith in God we can expect a return on our investment.

I had to make many investments stretched over a number of years. First of all, I had a plan to purchase a home for my child and I. I had a lot of money saved for the purchase, but I just could not seem to find the right home, and I have been searching for a couple of years. I thank God He allowed me to save my money obediently; however, I later realized the money would not be used for the purchase of a home. As much as I had a clear vision and expectation to win my case, the journey I planned to embark on towards my dream was not in the same vehicle God was leading me on. I was driving a Lamborghini and if felt like God had me on a 10 speed bike.

Understand that what you think are setbacks, are actually set ups. I needed to file an appeal on my case within less than one month from the previous ruling. I had to not only hire a new attorney, but pay for court records from the trial, and prepare to pay child support. My appeal alone exhausted my entire savings. At that point, the questions I asked earlier came back again, and I noticed panic tried to settle again in my spirit. I wondered again, "Lord, how am now going to survive? Am I making the right decision to appeal my case?" Then the questions changed to "Lord, what are you trying to show me? What must I do to make things better?" I stressed wondering if I could afford to even take care of myself.

My core at that time was not strong. God was trying to show me that He would not place anything before me that I could not bear (1 Corinthians 10:13). He was showing me that I had to trust Him. Although I said I did from my lips, my actions did not show it when venting to my parents and sister about this entire situation repeatedly. I think I may have stressed them out in the process.

I tried to let go of worrying to concentrate on things that mattered. But I was too invested in getting things done my way, you know the way I planned it in my head. I am a natural planner who operated on a timeframe. *When things did not occur in the order I planned it to, I tried to force it.* I am a very logical person, but logic got in the way of faith many times. The entire time, God was trying to show me that He would help me. I was confused in the meaning behind faith without works is dead, because I thought I had to do all of the work, and I eventually left the faith out unintentionally. If it was not for the fact that I was so meticulous and could not find a home I liked sooner, I probably would not have had enough money to file my appeal. I eventually paid the for the appeal, thankful that I had the money for it, but at the same time, I felt disappointed.

My friend Toni encouraged I journal and try to reflect on the positive things that were happening in my life. That helped because it forced me to think beyond my feelings and tap into a safe place, the truth. You see, it is so easy for us to dwell on the negative things when we are so afflicted and in our feelings because we may be fine today, but a few days later the pain may come back. I had to learn how to cope. Toni taught me that a way of coping was to point out all the good things God was doing for me. In that, it calmed me down and led me to pray. I later realized that God took care of my finances thereafter for me in ways I did not foresee. This helped me believe that God was with me and that His presence was not as far as I thought it was at times.

The more I began to grow spiritually, it was apparent to me that God specialized in an unequal fight for me. Just like the stories of David and Goliath and Moses freeing the Israelites, I too felt like I was fighting a battle outnumbered. You may have felt the same way at some point in your life. I caution you to not give up. Don't lose faith. God loves you, adores you, and will provide you with an escape plan.

UNWRAPPING FAITH

The fruit I am reminded of when I think of faith are lemons. Lemons, like faith are bitter sweet. Depending on how ripe lemons are, they may have a sweet or an extremely bitter flavor. Regardless, they provide benefits to the entire body, internally, externally, and are used for scents, drinking, and cooking. The development of the fruit takes time. Many people often have trouble producing fruit on their lemon trees because they are either not watering it enough, or that it has a poor rootstock. When care for the tree is neglected, the harvest will be few. Like faith, if we are not rooted in God through prayer, learning His word, and by obeying Him, we too will not reap any benefits by planting a seed on an unsoiled ground. It's not easy to walk in faith, but when we do, the outcome is sweet. The stronger our faith is, the stronger the root will become.

WE EXERCISE FAITH WHEN:

- We never lose sight of our vision.
- We no longer believe we are buried, but planted instead.
- We are able to trust that God has our back.

- We believe God will turn a hopeless situation into blessings beyond measure.
- Our expectations for what God can do for us will not cease.
- We can still move towards our vision.
- We're able to take risks after consulting with God.
- We realize our setback is our set up for success.
- We can make lemonade out of lemons!

CHAPTER 10

EXERCISING GENTLENESS

Each day I wake my son up in the morning to get ready for school, there is consistency in my tone as I kiss his cheek, caress his tummy, and sing in a soft and cheerful voice, "Good morning my little sweetie! It's mommy. Time to wake up." He responds in a slurred and exhausted voice, "Five more minutes, please?" And of course, my response is, "Sure baby." I tuck him back in and allow him his extra time, which is typically more than what he requested. I do this because I want him to wake up feeling loved and not rushed, although there are those occasional moments when we have overslept. Plus, I know that trying to pry a child away from the comfort of their bed can be challenging, therefore, I handle him with ease.

Gentleness is the next fruit of the spirit. For many years of my life, I related gentleness to being delicate, considerate and kind. I described a gentle person based on the type of care they provided to others. I was only able to see it from one perspective until I realized it is a character rich in value that God desires us to acquire. To fulfill my curiosity, I looked up gentleness and discovered that a gentle person exhibits the character of meekness, humility, gratitude, calmness, and tenderness (Colossians 3:12). This fruit is a very important example of how God envision us to be like. All of these characters surrounding gentleness make big impacts on others and ourselves. So how can we exercise gentleness in such a harsh world?

Gentleness is having an humble and meek attitude of wanting to help others instead of wanting to be superior to them. Gentle people have an authentic concern for the well-being of others instead of their own. If I gave you sixty seconds to list as many people you know who fit that description, how many people would you name? If I gave you two minutes to reflect on as many people you have encountered in your life who genuinely looked out for your well-being and did not even have to, could you name any? What could you produce if I gave you ten minutes to write down all of the things you have done for others within the last week, big or small, without expecting something back in return? It could be praying for people who did not ask for a prayer request, discretely putting in a good word for someone who needed a reference, offering a lift to a stranger when they were stranded, or even providing someone with honest and wise counsel when they needed advice. Yes, these are all examples of kind acts, but the intention and attitude displayed when providing them determine if they are made in gentle ways or not.

For example, I can be honest with someone, but in a brutal, and not gentle way. I can argue a point and justify it with several facts, but if my intention is to put someone down while making my point, I am not genuinely seeking their best interest. Instead, I entered a competitive match to prove how right my point of view is as opposed to theirs. 1 Peter 5:5 states that "God resists the proud, but gives grace to the humble" (NKJV). In many instances, it is not about being right. The delivery of how we express care and concern towards others is what matters. I've learned the best way to respond to people who may have a hot temper or who are prideful is by being gentle. Do I feel at times they deserve it? No. Do they need it? Yes. Modeling good behaviors is a better way to approach situations rather than telling people what they may already know about themselves.

Humility is a character that exudes self-control. Many people think humble people have low esteem and underestimate their importance. Would it make sense for God to want us to be undistinguished among others? Absolutely not! An humble person is not prideful nor arrogant. They are able to let petty things go by resisting arguments over trivial things to make a point, and they refrain from being boastful. Humble people are focused less on themselves and more on people around them, showing compassion and consideration towards others without seeking credit for themselves. A gentle and humble person is able to correct people without putting them down, comfort people even when they are wrong, and stand firm, yet controlled.

God

Many people do not realize how gentle God is each day, even when we make mistakes. His gentleness comes in the form of reminders, distractors, or caution when we least expect them. For instance, many of us have formed relationships with people we know we probably should have never dated. Because we were lonely, we entertained him or her. When we make decisions like that, God does not slap us on the head or call us dumb, although, if we are truthful, we can admit that we often make many unintelligent decisions. Instead, God gently provides us with signs that may reveal that person's "true character" to us. And He continues to do it. Some people take heed to them, while some acknowledge them, but still pursue the relationship. No matter how we respond, God continues to caution us in a loving manner.

We often make unsafe decisions each day. Have you ever texted, eaten, put on make-up, or even reached for something all while trying to drive? I'm guilty of that. While driving, have you ever dropped the tool you were using, such as a pen, eyeliner, cell phone, papers, food, etc... Why do you think this happened? From a logical standpoint, we can say it's from suddenly pumping the breaks or a distraction caused the items to fall. This may be true, but understand that God has control over all things. If I drop my eyeliner and I can no longer access it, then putting on make-up will have to be something to do after I reach a stopping point. This may be His gentle way of reminding us to focus on getting to the destination safely instead of trying to multi-task.

2 Samuel 22:36 states, "You have also given me the shield of your salvation; Your gentleness has made me great" (NKJV). Have you ever

encountered times when you became angry with someone and just as you were about to retaliate, God entered your thoughts and helped you resist the urge? Maybe you misinterpreted an email that was sent from your boss that you initially did not like. Due to preconceived frustrations, you respond to the email in an undiplomatic way, but just before you sent it, God cautioned you to calm down, let it go, and address the issue a different way. In many cases, God's gentleness has helped us learn from our mistakes and protect us from displaying a character that we may later regret.

Remember, we are representations of God. My parents used to tell us to not embarrass them around people. What they meant was they did not want us to act the fool because our actions are a reflection of how they raised us. We tell our own children the same thing. But how often do we hold ourselves accountable for our own character? When our flesh is willing to become self-righteous, call others out in harsh ways, and act superior towards others, as children of God, do we represent Him well? Do our actions match the character of Him? Self-reflection should be a daily assignment we never take for granted. As tomorrow is not promised to us, we also do not know what circumstances we will face; therefore, we must exercise Godly character daily to strengthen our core.

Our Savior Rejected by a Samaritan Village

Be honest. Have you ever had a good day and was in an awesome mood, then suddenly, you unexpectantly stumbled across someone who was rude to you? You're minding your business, being friendly, and when you say hello to them, they roll their eyes at you or simply don't respond. How about times when you received rude service at a supermarket, the mechanic shop, or on a customer service phone call? When we encounter rudeness, it is likely that we somehow feel rejected, which is a hurtful feeling that may cause us to retaliate.

Luke 9 (51-56) describes a moment when Jesus and His disciples were rejected as they entered a Samaritan village while traveling to Jerusalem after a long journey of healing many people. When they arrived in the Samaritan village, the Samaritans did not receive them because they knew Jesus and His disciples were headed towards Jerusalem. When Jesus' disciples, James and John saw this, they got offended and wanted to retaliate by saying, "Lord, do You want us to command fire to come down from heaven and consume them, just as Elijah did?" (verse 54, NKJV).

Jesus' disciples were highly offended and knew they had leverage to command fire down from heaven and destroy them; however, Jesus asserts in a gentle way that this behavior would contradict the character God wants them to portray. I'm quite sure Jesus was thinking, "Have you lost your minds?" They have been preaching the gospel and healing many people and although the Samaritan people are not showing favor towards them, seeking revenge would contradict everything they have preached so far. Instead, Jesus rebuked James and John, and then stated, "You do not know what manner of spirit you are of. For the Son of Man did not come to destroy men's lives but to save *them*" (Luke 9:55-56, NKJV). At that point, I could imagine they were tired and frustrated; however, they continued their journey to another village peacefully.

Proverbs 15:1 states, "A soft answer turns away wrath, but a harsh word stirs up anger" (NKJV). Sometimes it's best to swallow your pride and keep it moving instead of challenge every fight. Some people may think a gentle person is weak, but they exude strength in self-control. It's okay for us to be strong in our beliefs, but we must proceed with wisdom, caution, and show love when expressing our concerns.

GOD TEACHES US IN MOMENTS OF WEAKNESS

Shortly after I filed my appeal, I made a risky decision without seeking God's approval. I knew that unethical alliances were formed against me through the court that hindered me from winning my custody case, so I found a way to retrieve email conversations from the parties involved as a way to gather evidence for my appeal. I knew it was the wrong thing to do, and God was gently trying to get my attention the entire time by warning me that I could get caught and face heavy consequences. However, I was desperate, ignored the signs, and fell under the curiosity of finding the evidence I knew existed and the intrinsic pressure I placed on myself to fight for primary custody of my child.

I was able to retrieve what I needed for a while, but eventually was caught and under an investigation. Even in doing something wrong, I compared my wrongdoing to others. I wondered why *I* got caught after I did *one* thing wrong, while others were permitted to get away with deceit. I caused more stress on top of the emotional distress I faced from my custody case.

I later learned as unfair as it was that two wrongs did not make a right. I leaned on my intuition instead of asking God for discernment. Our intuition helps us identify something without conscious reasoning through instinct feelings. Discernment is knowing what's good or bad based on God's word. I knew what was wrong, I just neglected to be patient and trust God to handle things the way He wanted to. God saw in my actions that I still did not have faith in Him. If I did, I would have waited on Him to take vengeance, for the scriptures says, "vengeance is mine, and recompense; their foot shall slip in *due* time" (Deuteronomy 32:35, NKJV). Instead, I had to correct a new problem I created by hiring a criminal attorney, admit to my fault before the judge, pay probation fines and work several hours of probation.

While all of this was happening, life still rolled on. I still worked full time, was committed to a ministry at church, went to graduate school full time, and raised my child as a single mother. During this time, I still had to interact with people, work to my fullest potential, and remain disciplined in my studies. It was not easy. When we find ourselves in situations where we feel we have been dealt a bad hand, it is hard to keep our composure. It's easy to be mad at the world, throw a pity party, not be helpful to others and not be our best self. I had to learn to not take my frustrations out on people around me. I knew there was still so much to gain, and I couldn't advance if I ruined relationships with people around me nor if I slacked professionally. I tried to stay prayerful and hopeful that something good would eventually transpire.

Gentleness is being willing to accept limitations without taking frustrations out on others. That takes a lot of self-control. Trust me, we can't keep our anger and aggravations bottled up inside. They must come out! Anytime I felt annoyed, I would call someone I trusted to just vent to or I cried out to God. I tried my best to not allow others to provoke me. I continued to journal and found myself trying to recommit to goals I previously set. As I listed things I was grateful for, I realized my father, someone who warned me initially to be careful in each decision I made and always referenced God, never criticized me nor disrespected me for the irrational decisions I made. I'm quite sure he was worried about me and was not happy, but he was always firm when he spoke to me. His approach was gentle enough for me to listen. I learned in return to aim to be that way.

Gentle teachings from The Apostle Paul

The Apostle Paul treated people with gentleness. He was caring and loved the Lord so much that he did all he could to lead people towards the truth. Even those who were misguided or under false teachings, Paul had a way of being passionate and bold, yet gentle towards them when trying to explain to them the truth about God. Paul was a teacher. And if you know anything about the job of teaching, coaching, or even parenting, it can be a frustrating task to exert so much time and effort to prepare and communicate messages to help people grow, especially if they do not take them seriously or are still confused about what you're trying to convey. When frustrated and under pressure, it's easy to become less delicate, and become more harsh.

In Chapter 3, *Exercising Love*, I mentioned that love is patient and kind. That means when we genuinely have the heart and desire to help others, we must do so without expecting to receive credit, even if those we try to help do not appreciate it, understand why, or show gratitude at that very moment. We must learn to not allow the behaviors of others to influence how we behave. We should allow the Holy Spirit to guide us in every decision we make. The more we condition our minds to think this way, we allow ourselves more opportunities to show gentleness. 1 Corinthians 4:21 states, "Which do you choose? Should I come with a rod to punish you, or should I come with love and a gentle spirit?" (NLT). I'm quite sure many of us would want to be treated with love and gentleness instead of being punished with a rod. "Do unto others as you would have them do" (Luke 6:31, NIV).

In Acts 17 (1-34), the Apostle Paul and his companions traveled through many cities. In Thessalonica, Paul spent a few days preaching and proving that Jesus, the Messiah had to suffer, die, and rise from the dead. Those whom Paul was able to persuade joined him, while many Jews became jealous, formed a mob, and then started a riot. Paul and those who believed him traveled to Berea, and then Athens, continuing to preach the word of God.

Upon their arrival to Athens, Paul was disappointed and upset to see the city was full of idols. He did his best to reason with Greeks and Jews in the synagogue who believed in and loved God regarding his concern. Instead of Paul making accusations or throwing harsh criticism towards them, he eased people away from the idea of worshipping several gods and towards worshipping the one true God. He began in verses 22-23 by acknowledging how religious they are and specifically that they worshipped an unknown God. The way he drove his point was to have them reflect on the fact that they worship an unknown god and not worship a one and only God who made the world and everything in it.

After he was able to get their attention, he made points that were based on relevant facts that supported his argument. Imagine if Paul chastised them by saying, "Fools! You are such sinners worshipping outrageous gods! You hypocrites better pray you don't get struck down!" Would he gain any favor? Would anyone be willing to follow him, a person with character such as that? Probably not.

Paul was stern and forthright. He wasn't the type of teacher who delivered information and kept it moving regardless if it was received or not. He encouraged those who did well and motivated those who did not understand. He genuinely cared about helping people understand what God desired of them and had them repent from their mistakes. Sometimes, when we're passionate about helping others, we must be cognizant on how we deliver the message. A person full of knowledge and skill can be the biggest turn off if their attitude is prideful, provocative, and rude.

Did Paul gain everyone's attention? Most of them. Did they all agree with him? No. We must understand that we cannot control the outcome of others. We can only control our actions. Isaiah 50:4 states, "The Sovereign LORD HAS GIVEN ME A WELL-INSTRUCTED TONGUE, to know the word that sustains the weary. He wakens me morning by morning, wakens my ear to listen like one being instructed" (NIV). As long as we remain focused on God, whatever goal we want to accomplish can be achieved, and God will continue to bless us with the unimaginable because we chose to be obedient to the spirit and not the flesh.

Meekness in Moses

To be gentle is also to me meek and calm. A meek person is obedient and submissive to the Lord. They have a quiet and calm trust in God to the point where they are willing to do whatever He commands and refrain from revenge and defensiveness even when they are right. That is tough for many to do! From childhood, we are taught to stand up for ourselves. Growing up with siblings, we were often blamed for doing something we didn't do. It is very hard to not retaliate when we feel we are under attack. It's okay to protect ourselves, but how we go about doing that makes a big difference.

We must choose our battles wisely. If someone started a rumor against you that you were a liar, if you know that is not your character and you do not have a history of getting in the middle of drama, people will most likely not believe it anyway. Your character spoke for itself. Those who believed it *wanted* to. It's not your responsibility to force someone to like you or think a certain way of you. The truth will always come to the light.

In Numbers 12, Moses' character spoke for itself when his siblings, Miriam and Aaron spoke badly against him. Moses was aware of it, and so was God. Instead of lashing back at them, Moses was able to absorb adversity and criticism and refrain from being defensive. Instead of saying anything, Moses waited patiently on God. Numbers 12:3 states, ("Now Moses was a very humble man, more humble than anyone else on the face of the Earth") (NIV). Being meek, humble, or gentle is not a term we describe just anyone. It is a character that is earned. The scripture defines Moses as more humble than any man on Earth. Because of this, God came to his rescue and vindicated Moses in front of his siblings.

MEEKNESS

A meek person is able to learn. In order to learn, we must we willing to be taught, free from distractions. If we feel the need to talk over people, we're not listening. Silent and listen are spelled with the same letters. In order to be taught, we must be reflective and willing to receive information even if we do not agree with it. Does it make us gullible? Of course not. Does it mean we can get upset inside? We sure can. We're human. It means we must learn to be slow to anger and be able to control our actions.

In the past, I will admit that it offended me when people referred to me as meek. At that time, I was unsure what meekness meant. I assumed that because I was reserved, people saw me as a pushover, or someone not to be taken seriously. We live in a society where people feel the more dramatic we are, the more interesting we are, or the feistier or "shadier" we are, the more respect we earn. Many of society's expectations to even be successful is to lie our way to the top. I think it's crazy that we operate in such dysfunction, yet alone crave drama! I never wanted to be the person people could not respect or rely on. I feel I have some meek and gentle qualities, but I'm definitely no Moses!

Over the past few years, I feel that my character has been under a lengthy test. God is using me for a higher purpose and He has a mighty way of showing it! I had to learn how to be meek and calm in addition to many other spiritual fruit throughout my custody process. Through all of this, I have been prompted to exercise my core. Even as I write this chapter, I am being tested on how gentle I am towards people. God is so real and instead of allowing the enemy to provoke me, I am trying my best to focus on God's plan for me. I must admit, I feel like I suffer many days. It is a struggle for me to deny the flesh- not feel compelled to justify every lie or even retaliate. It's difficult, but Romans 8:36-37 provided me with helpful insight, "For Your sake we are being put to death all day long; we were considered as sheep to be slaughtered. But in all these things we overwhelmingly conquer through Him who loved us" (NASB).

Gentleness requires the existence of love. One cannot be gentle and not loving. Gentle people show gratitude for small things and tolerance for those who do not serve us well. Yes, I said tolerance! Paul was tolerant to the many people he preached to. Moses was tolerant towards his siblings. Jesus was tolerant to His disciples. Throughout the bible, the Apostle Paul gave great prescriptions for healthy relationships. Let's keep it real, it seems to be impossible to have decent relationships with everyone, let alone get along with everyone. But Paul wrote in Romans 12:18, "If possible, so far as it depends on you, be at peace with all men" (NASB). Treating even the most tempered person with gentleness may change how they relate to you for the better. We must live as those made alive in Christ. Therefore, we should resist the flesh, be slow to speak, quick to listen, and purify our hearts and thoughts (Colossians 3:1-11).

UNWRAPPING GENTLENESS

In this world, gentle people are often underestimated; however, their quiet spirit is widely impacted. A fruit that has this same effect are kiwi. Let's be real, the hairy brown exterior is not very flattering, let alone does not make my mouth water. When I was younger, I never desired kiwi just because of how they look. But, as many people say, never judge a book by its' cover! When I got older and began to experiment more with different types of food, I fell in love with the kiwi flavor.

Kiwi is a fruit that is handled gently, because its' flesh is very thin. In addition, by eating the skin of kiwi, the fiber intake triples. Kiwi is also known to induce sleep, provide beautiful skin, and is loaded with antioxidants and minerals. Just as we must be delicate with the kiwi when picking or storing them to receive all of the wonderful benefits the fruit has to offer, we must be gentle to others so they can receive the great gift God has to offer them. The act of being thoughtful, strong, respectful, humble, kind and loving will help us sleep at night, age appropriately, and restore our health because we are less likely to worry nor stress about things we have no control of.

Know that it's okay to be the kiwi- gentle. We do not have to fit in to what society picture us to be like. Live the way God created us to live.

WE ARE EXERCISING GENTLENESS WHEN:

- We apologize quickly after we make emotional outbursts.
- We seek to settle differences in a reasonable way.
- We are quick to listen, and slow to speak.
- We remind ourselves how gentle God is to us.
- We are wise and loving in expressing our beliefs.
- We are cognizant of what we say and how it may affect others, even if it is giving advice or constructive criticism.

Remember, meekness is not weakness! Gentleness is strength in self-control. When you find yourself feeling weak, allow God to be strong within you. Seek Him and allow Him to guide you.

CHAPTER 11

EXERCISING SELF-CONTROL

Just as a meek person can control his/her behavior and attitude, a person with self-restraint has the ability to control his/her level of pride, appetite, and temper. The ninth and last fruit of the spirit is self-control. Each day, our flesh produce desires that should be denied or controlled. According to Luke 9:23, we should deny ourselves and take up our cross daily. A person with self-control is able to maintain moderation and control over daily temptations.

Are you a coffee drinker? If so, I agree it can be difficult saying "no" to your morning coffee. I personally, don't drink a lot of it each morning, but having it available to sip on the entire morning brings me comfort. I literally may only drink one-fourth of my thermos, so while I naturally like the taste of coffee, the idea of having it determines my mood.

We are often able to control many temptations through our minds. As I mentioned before in Chapter 1, *Exercising Your Mind*, there are three main functions of our minds. They are thinking, feeling, and wanting. We often think about things we do not need, and because it is on our mind, we develop feelings and want it. Each day, our flesh generates several wants. They are often random and unpredictable. For instance, I may not be hungry, but rest assure, if someone enter the room with a Chick-Fil-A sandwich and waffle fries, I can suddenly taste the fries dipped in honey mustard sauce. After thinking of it for a while, my mind will persuade me to go to Chick-Fil-A for lunch.

Food is a big temptation. For those of us who have fasted, the temptation is so real on the first two days of fasting. We find ourselves circling he kitchen, looking into refrigerators and pantries only because we have conditioned our minds on what is deprived rather than directing our focus on positive things. That's how we are when we face problems. We replay it repeatedly in our minds to either develop solutions or because we entered panic and stress mode. Hebrews 12:11 states, "No discipline seems pleasant at the time, but painful. Later on; however, it produces a harvest of righteousness and peace for those who have been trained by it" (NIV). If we do not have self-control, we will become enslaved by what controls us. It is interesting how we can find ourselves dependent on things such as coffee to kick start our day. Where is God in our list of daily needs?

Jesus Tempted in the Wilderness

In Luke 4:1-13, Jesus was tempted in the wilderness by Satan. Before I even get into the scriptures, being tempted in such a vulnerable place- the wilderness- is such a crafty move by Satan. What's in the wilderness? Lack of food and water, which are essentials we need to live. With little of it, we find ourselves easily distracted. Our minds begin to play tricks on us because it's being fueled by the desires of our flesh.

However, Jesus was in the wilderness after fasting from food for forty days and was extremely hungry. Low and behold, He was approached by the devil who challenged Jesus to prove that He is the Son of God by turning a stone into bread. Although Jesus' stomach was empty from food, it is stated in verse 1 that Jesus was filled with the Holy Spirit. He responded in verse 4, "…Man shall not live on bread alone" (NIV).

Of course, the devil made more advances towards Jesus. Have you felt this way? Suppose you decided to become more God-like in your character and grow a stronger relationship with God. At the same time, your patience has been tested by people, you may have entered a trial, and here comes Satan. Your mind tells you that you are frustrated, and because aggravation is on your mind, it takes everything within you to not lash out on people. Self-control is not about bringing ourselves under our own control. It's about surrendering to Christ.

As Satan approached Jesus again, he led Him to a high place where they could oversee the city below them. He tried to bargain with Jesus that if He worshipped Satan, he would give Him all splendor and authority. Jesus held firm to His belief and told him to only worship and serve God. After the devil made a third unsuccessful attempt towards Jesus, he fled until he saw another opportune time. If the flesh was allowed to have it's way, it would lead us into worse conditions. Because my flesh was curious, as I stated in Chapter 10, it led me to paying probation fees and working volunteer hours. We have a way of over worrying, over working, and overindulging to the point where we no longer walk by faith. We essentially create and walk by the beat of our own drum. When we allow ourselves to be controlled by the Holy Spirit, we allow God to produce discipline within us that will keep us physically strong and moderately balanced.

Joseph and Potiphar's Wife

In Chapter 6, *Exercising Patience (Longsuffering)*, I described Joseph's journey through longsuffering and faithfulness in God. Not only was Joseph patient, he was a man who exercised an abundance of self-control. Genesis 39 depicts the story about the handsome and well-built Joseph whom was bought into slavery by a wealthy man named Potiphar. Joseph was a very hard worker and his service earned him a promotion as controller of Potiphar's house. The Lord was with Joseph because of his strong faith in Him. Potiphar saw God's favor over Joseph, which caused him to trust Joseph.

Just as things began to work in Joseph's favor, Potiphar's wife tempted him. Can you relate to this? Just as things are going well, the devil suddenly attempts to distract us and rob us from our happiness. When we are unable to control the new desires our flesh generate, we can prevent unwanted distractions from attacking our peace. This is what happened to Joseph. 1 Thessalonians 5:6 states, "So then, let us not be like others, who are asleep, but let us be awake and sober" (NIV). Joseph resisted sexual temptation from Potiphar's wife.

What I admire about Joseph's mindset was that he not only did not want to disrespect Potiphar, but in verse 9, he asked, "How can I do such a wicked thing and sin against God?" (NIV). It is often when we are tempted by anything, we first consider our environment or what's directly in front of us. God wants us to consider Him first. That's how we build strong character in Him. Children have a natural loyalty and dependency towards their parents. When they are faced with temptation, they mostly refer to their parent's expectations before making their decisions. For instance, before they sneak a piece of cake, misbehave at school, or sneak out of the house, they think about the consequence of getting caught by their parent, but also know they do not want to disappoint them. Somehow, after we reach adulthood, we feel liberated and totally independent that although our conscious warns right from wrong, our minds tell us that we are capable of doing what we want. This is a dangerous way of thinking because when we disconnect from the spirit and are led by the flesh, we find ourselves facing hardships we could have avoided.

An important point I want to make about Joseph's noble decision to resist Potiphar's wife's advances is that even when we make the right decisions, people may still retaliate against us. Sometimes, people who do not exercise Godly conduct will allow their flesh to tempt them into seeking vengeance against those who denied them. This is what happened to Joseph. After Joseph denied another attempt to sleep with her, she accused Joseph of making sexual advances towards her to the household servants and Potiphar.

Potiphar was surprised and grew angry toward Joseph, for he believed his deceitful wife. Consequently, Joseph was placed in prison and confined. Talk about unfair! Do you recall experiencing moments like this in your life? Have you encountered someone who has been either untruthful or even unfaithful to you and the moment you questioned him or her, they cast blame on *you*? "Have a good conscience, so that, when you are slandered, those who revile your good behavior in Christ may be put to shame" (1 Peter 3:16, ESV). Matthew 5:11 states, "Blessed are you when others revile you and persecute you and utter all kinds of evil against you falsely on my account" (ESV).

Joseph exercised a great deal of self-control. Even after he was falsely accused, convicted and sentenced to prison, the scriptures plainly indicate in verses 20-21 that the Lord was still with him. Even in prison, the warden saw favor in Joseph and put him in charge of the prison. No matter where Joseph was, even if it seemed bad through the lens of his flesh, God ensured success followed Joseph!

What we think, say, and do are all areas involving self-control.

It's not easy to resist temptation. When attempting to adjust our temperament or refrain from certain behaviors or habits, our bodies create withdrawal symptoms. When it's not accustomed to something new, it has to work harder to adjust to it. It's like exercising for the first time. After the first few days of working out, the body feels tired. It's not used to exerting as much energy. When more energy is exerted, the body needs more fuel and rest. So do not expect to see changes over night. Just as the body has needs, so does the spirit. When trying to strengthen our core through self-control, we must expect to increase our prayer time, become edified with the word of God, and encounter discomfort. Self-control helps us resist something now for something greater in the future.

OPPOSITON IN THE MIDST OF RESISTING

I got to a point where I learned to do my best to take care of myself physically, emotionally, and spiritually. It was not easy for me to focus on myself, especially when I was so used to focusing on helping people around me and commit to my studies at the same time. My spiritual health was a challenge many times. The more I tried to live by God's word, the more opposition I seemed to face.

I felt like my patience was always a test! The more I endured; my physical health took a toll on me and I began to feel drained. I remained optimistic, because instead of focusing on when things would shift in my life or even how, I reflected on what God has blessed me with so far. Of course, when I shifted my mindset to being positive, more adversity came my way.

Shortly after surprising our father with his 60th birthday party, we soon discovered he was diagnosed with a cancer called multiple myeloma. From that point on, my sole responsibility in conjunction to raising my son was to learn about this disease, comfort my father, and provide him with the best health care at the best facility. The hard part was watching my father endure so much pain many times. There were moments when I wanted to question God, yet again. I did not understand why each year it seemed I faced a new challenge.

I was angry. And hurt. There were times I did not want to pray, foolishly. But let's get real, that was when I needed God the most. "The Lord is not slow in keeping his promise, as some understand slowness. Instead he is patient with you, not wanting anyone to perish, but everyone to come to repentance" (2 Peter 3:9, NIV). I saw that even in moments when I thought things around me was so unfair that God was disciplining me. The scripture advises us to, "Endure hardships as discipline; God is treating you as sons. For what son is not disciplined by his father?" (Hebrews12:5-7, NIV). If He did not care, he would let me walk into danger. I see now He was patient with me and that I had to step outside of my problems and be helpful towards those who needed me the most. I loved caring for my father. We had many great moments during treatment, especially when we things were looking great.

About seven months after my father's diagnosis, his battle with cancer ended. This truly broke me to pieces. I felt let down because I held on to hope and knew my father's health would restore. I experienced loss for so long and feelings of unfairness rose in my spirit… yet again. But something unexpected happened. The week of my father's passing, although I was hurt and stressed from people around me, I felt a huge sense of peace. It was weird. I never in a million years thought I would be so composed at a time like that. The scripture, "… and the peace of God, which surpasses all understanding, will guard your hearts and minds in Christ Jesus" (Philippians 4:7, ESV) suddenly became so real to me. Yes, I faced work, graduate school, and family-related distractions, but I had inner peace of mind knowing my father was in a better place. I miss him dearly, but anytime I think of him, God gently allow him to appear in my dreams, my thoughts and my memories. All so pleasant. At that point, I realized I was growing. And it felt good.

God is with me. When I anticipated I would not be able to compose myself if I ever lost a parent, God gave me self-control. We often underestimate ourselves and our abilities to do things. Incredible things. But Philippians 4:13 states, "I can do all things through Christ who strengthens me" (NKJV).

UNWRAPPING SELF-CONTROL

As you can probably tell, I love fruit. I can eat an entire fruit platter filled with cantaloupe, pineapples, blue berries, strawberries, and grapes in one day. Although fruit has many health benefits, when we modify our fruit by adding chocolate syrup, strawberry dip, and caramel to them, we cancel some of the rich and organic benefits it has to offer for something of no nutritional value.

Every fruit comes to my mind when I think of self-control. Why? Because in order to have self-control, we must exercise a portion of each fruit of the spirit. We must love ourselves and others enough to resist the flesh. We must show kindness to control our anger towards others. We must lean on God's understanding rather than our own. Any resistance of our flesh requires putting others before our wants.

We can't modify love, joy, peace, longsuffering, kindness, goodness, faith and gentleness. It reminds me of many friends I have who aim to eat healthy, so they're excited in the beginning of their health journey to eat fruit, veggies and protein. But they are put to the test when they can no longer add the three cheeses, bacon bits, ham, eggs, chicken, avocado, and croutons to their kale and spinach mix nor drench it with dressing each time they eat their salad. It tastes great with all of the extra toppings, but when we give in to the gratification and impulse of eating a tasty salad for that moment, we deny ourselves the greater reward in the future. We must exercise Godly character through the nourishment of spiritual fruit in it's most authentic form- the way God intended. God tests our character in moments when we least expect it. That's when good exercise occurs.

It may be safe to suggest that our biggest enemy is often ourselves. We get in the way of our own success when we rely solely on own thoughts and feelings in the midst of making decisions. One question I recommend we ask when determining if we are practicing self-control is: Is our flesh or is our spirit running the show? Below are some tips you may use to determine if you are exercising self-control.

WE EXERCISE SELF-CONTROL WHEN:

- We are able to control our temper.
- We are able to not lash out at people when things to not do go as planned.
- We are able to control our urges when people disrespect us.
- Others can describe us as calm and collected individuals.
- Our first reaction to something is to exercise a fruit of the spirit and resist the flesh.
- We don't always have to have the last word.
- We can let go of pettiness.

It takes work to have self-control. Nevertheless, it will always feel like work when we force disciplined behavior rather than seek God. Allow Him to change your heart. The outcome is worth the exercise.

CHAPTER 12

BENEFITS OF FRUIT

God's presence is so beneficial. Everything we do should be centered on God's divine purpose. If you are pursuing a companion, your goal may be to win her heart. If you are trying to start a business, you may want to accompany people who are business owners. If you want to lose weight, you may consult with a personal trainer. If you want to build your credit, a financial adviser may help. My point is that all we try to possess on Earth are things that may sustain us while we are here. When we want something, we pursue it. If we want to be like Christ, we should produce the character of Him. We claim we are Christians and want to live abundantly, but somehow forget to report to the One who can make it happen for us. He is God.

Remember, the fruit does not only benefit us, but those around us. Think of yourself as a change agent. We want to spread God's love to all we encounter each day. When trying to nurture our character, it is important we reference God and acknowledge those who have modeled to us the character we want to acquire. In Romans 16, the Apostle Paul took time to reference to all of those who have been fruitful to him throughout his life. Think about some moments in your life when individuals (people you know or strangers) have rescued you, offered to help you, given you advice, prayed for you, were truthful with you, or even taught you. Do you ever acknowledge people who has helped you in moments when you needed them, or do you just take them for granted?

Personal Greetings from the Apostle Paul

In Romans 16, Paul puts things into perspective. He began by commending Phoebe, a deacon of a church in Cenchreae for being such a bold, yet *kind* person. Paul trusted her to deliver his letter to the Romans. Priscilla and Aquila, a married couple Paul referenced, were co-workers in Christ Jesus (Romans 16:1-4). Paul described them as individuals who risked their lives for him. That is how *loving* they were. One can infer that if they risked their lives for Paul, then Aquila would have risked his life for his wife. "Husbands, love your wives, just as Christ loved the church and gave Himself for her" (Ephesians 5:25, NIV).

Throughout this chapter, Paul encouraged readers to greet the individuals he acknowledged. Paul wanted them to be accepted and received into fellowship because we are one in Christ. In Romans 16:5-16, Paul referenced several more people, many by name. Paul was a busy man who traveled and spread the word of God. However, he stopped to reflect and encourage greetings among so many different people, men and women, rich and poor, servants and leaders, and Gentiles and Jews. Galatians 3:26-27 states, "For you are all sons of God through faith in Christ Jesus. For all of you who were baptized into Christ have clothed yourselves with Christ" (NASB).

HARMONY

One of the biggest benefits of the fruit of the spirit is harmony. God wants us to make Him our priority so that we can love and serve others, putting their interest above ours. Offer up to God those who have touched us and those we have influenced for their good. Romans 14:19 states, "So then let us pursue what makes for peace and for mutual upbuilding" (ESV). It wears and tears on our hearts, minds, and spirit when we feud with others. It leads to worry, sometimes paranoia, stress, and it distracts us from focusing and being productive. If we are unwise in our battles, we spread our drama through gossip, forming alliances against people, and feed into negative energy. In Romans 12:16-18, we are instructed to "Live in harmony with one another. Do not be haughty, but associate with the lowly. Never be wise in your own sight. Repay no one evil for evil, but give thought to do what is honorable in the sight of all. If possible, so far as it depends on you, live peaceably with all" (ESV).

LEARNING HOW TO Ex-E-R-C-I-S-E OUR CORE

You may be wondering what to do when life tests your character. As many of us know, most of our training goes out of the window when life put us to the test. To avoid this from happening, I created an Ex-E-R-C-I-S-E model, designed to help us self-reflect on our goals, our thoughts, and how to respond in any situation.

Explore- Explore the word of God. Be around God-like people and learn from their testimonies. Pray without ceasing. Ask the following questions: Am I searching for answers in the wrong places? Am I spending quiet time with God? Do I understand what is happening in my life? Have I laid my concerns at the alter? How can I be obedient? How can I be wise?

Expect- Expect some things in your life to shift beyond your control. Not all change is bad, even if it is unexpected. Be optimistic. Be open to change. Take control of the things you can change and make a plan. You can't expect goals to be achieved if they aren't created. Assess your circle of friends, your habits, and how you spend your time. Take those things into consideration when constructing your plan. However, include God in your plan. Make sure it is His will and not your own.

Reflect- You've listened to God, wrote down goals, so now it's time to reflect on your character. Think about changes you're making to handle trials. Would God be proud of your decisions or behavior?

Do people see growth in you? Are you still able to bless others when things aren't going as planned for you? Hold yourself accountable. Being accountable is refraining from making excuses and finger pointing. We are constantly evolving and growing to be better.

Commit- After you have reflected on your actions, recharge and commit to the sacrifices you planned to make. Focus on whether or not you are consistent with your actions towards being a better person. Be honest with yourself. Make no excuses.

Start a journal and vacation there occasionally. Pour out your heart on paper. It's safer to do it there. When you find yourself getting impatient and aggravated, pray and read scriptures. Read previous journal entries and evaluate any changes you've made. This will also help you reflect on wonderful things that has happened in your life thus far and allow you to renew your mindset.

Challenge yourself to push towards the finish line instead of quitting when frustrated. Commit to being encouraging to others as often as you can. Make decisions that are centered around God's will. Each day, ask yourself: Which fruit will I represent today?

Integrity- Our character will be tested here. Refrain from gossip as it comes to you. Be loyal. Be fair. Make wise decisions. Be honest. Follow the Golden Rule by treating others as you want to be treated. Stand up for what is wrong with an even temper.

Prepare yourself for the personalities of others. Many people are not committed to growing their character nor are even aware of theirs. Know the company you keep. If you are forced to interact with people who lack integrity, refrain from entertaining their antics. Don't jeopardize your character to prove a point. Be ethical and morally correct. Allow the light within you to reflect and your actions be the example- a positive one.

Sacrifice- Sacrifice more. The stronger your core becomes, the more you may need to sacrifice, especially if this is your season of longsuffering. Practice self-control by sacrificing fleshly desires to accommodate the spirit. Ignore petty arguments. Eliminate bad habits. Be available to others.

Start a spiritual fast. Enter a period of total submission. Sacrifice may mean we must grow in discomfort. Be prepared and equip yourselves with the full armor of God (Ephesians 6:10-18).

Endure- Never give up. Count your blessings and be thankful. Know that God will never leave you nor forsake you. He has brought you too far to leave you, so never leave Him.

In the process, you may get tired and frustrated, but they who wait on the Lord shall renew their strength (Isaiah 40). Your strength will be renewed and through God.

It's work, but the more you practice, the better you will get, and the greater the reward you will obtain.

I Explored

I too had to learn how to Ex-E-R-C-I-S-E. I will admit that I can be stubborn at times. I like to work out, but only within my own expectation and regimen. At the most, whenever I work out, I exercise about 10-15 minutes maximum. But, if I wanted to get my body all the way right, I know I would have to exert more discipline, time, and rigor in my exercise regimen.

I did not realize God was aiming to strengthen my character until a few years ago. My character was not bad, but God is preparing me for a higher purpose beyond what I can imagine. Once I realized that, I began to Ex-E-R-C-I-S-E. When I began to experience hardships, I began to pray. I prayed when I was upset. I prayed when I felt things were unfair. I prayed when I was confused. It seemed to be the only thing I could do within my control. I prayed often to simply vent.

I'll admit that sometimes, I got tired of praying especially when my prayers were self-centered. I cried- a lot. So praying at times made me feel sad. When I did not pray, I wrote journal entries and letters to God. My entries interestingly showed thanks to God. It helped me shift my mindset. Suddenly, each prayer became less about complaints and more about seeking God for clarification. I needed to be fixed.

That's when I began to read scriptures and daily inspiration books. I needed motivation. I also joined a ministry. There I was, broken and torn. I needed help, but was led to help others. God has given me urges to join a ministry two years prior to me initiating any moves. When I did, I was persistent in taking the initial step. I finally became obedient and listened. I gave more of myself when I felt that I needed a break or alone time. Sometimes we do, but always remember that God will surround us with people that will help bring out the best in us. Soon after, each journal entry became more about giving God gratification and glory in the midst of each challenge.

I Expected

I had no choice but to expect changes to occur. It was already happening. Despite of how things looked like on the outside, I had to accept what was happening, be open to changes, and most importantly be optimistic. I knew I physically did nothing wrong, so there had to be a higher purpose for why I encountered what I did.

I also expected God to turn my situation around. My expectation still stands today. As I lived through my trials, of course, resentment lingered and I felt saddened at times. But the feelings were temporary. They did not shut me out. I had to set goals and devise a plan. My friend Toni introduced me to vision boards. I created one and allowed it to help me stay on track.

Even after goal-setting, I had to learn to not expect every door to open. There were many that shut in my face. I learned to be wise enough to expect some failure, and never foolish enough to consider myself a failure. Clinging on to God helped me turn some failures into success.

I *Reflected*

I did a lot of reflecting. Sometimes, we just need to. My reflections were focused on things around me- things I've overcome and things I was striving to accomplish. I listed all of the events that took place in each year. I referred to my journal and amazingly, my entries reminded me of the many things God has blessed me with that I took for granted. Because I only focused on the big problems, I inadvertently neglected to absorb the small things He allowed me to overcome along the way.

Then I began to focus on my character. It started small- with continual gratification and then I learned about the fruit of the spirit. I instantly gravitated to patience (longsuffering) and faith. Why? Because I felt they were most relevant to me. I was curious to learn if I was being faithful to God. I also wondered why my season of wait was so long.

I chose to channel my energy on handling frustrations better. When a door shut in my face, I learned to not take it out on others. When others had good news, I wanted to be happy for them. In fact, I wanted to be in their circle so blessings could pour my way! I tried to be around God-fearing people who battled and overcame the same things I was going through. They may have not had the same problems, but they endured patience. My reflections led me to making small changes that produced big outcomes. I took accountability for making changes. It was up to me to take hold of the fruit and allow it to nurture me.

I *Committed*

I could no longer place blame on others. I could no longer make excuses for my actions. I could no longer back out. The race had already begun. God had big plans for me. Therefore, I made commitments. I chose to be the change I wanted to see in others. I committed to new fruit. Some weeks, I committed to self-control, while other weeks,

I committed to kindness or goodness. I even made them tangible by eating the fruit I wanted to exemplify each day such as apples (goodness) or pineapples (kindness). It helped me mentally believe that if I, for instance, poured goodness into body, the goodness within me would show, just like the expression, you are what you eat. As silly as it sounds, the actual fruit I ate held me accountable to that character. Plus, I enjoyed eating them!

Did it help my problems go away? No. However, it helped me handle them better. I worried less, stressed less, and was calmer. There were many times when I thought I faced a problem, instead of allowing it to bring me down, I put it aside and it worked itself out! How did that happen? When I no longer put my paws on it, God's healing hands covered it.

I delve into different fruit often. I can never get enough peaches (peace) or apples (goodness) or even the entire platter! I never stop learning about character and refining my own. Do not feel you have to completely understand each character. A wife or husband never know all they need to know about marriage. They learn during the process. A parent never knows everything they need to know about raising children. We live and learn along the way, but remain committed to the process. Life's challenges and personal experiences will be your best field trip as long as you allow God to be your teacher.

I held my Integrity

I tried my best to avoid intentional distractions. When I received messages or email from individuals who love to create arguments, I stopped reading them at work, when my child was around, or when I was busy. I stopped providing urgency to people who did not seek my best interest. I waited until my mind was focused, and I handled them on my own time. In many cases, I simply did not read them nor respond if I felt the nature of the conversation was to provoke me into an argument.

It took me a while to realize this worked for me because in the past, I felt the need to justify my point and prove myself against allegations made towards me. I've heard that curiosity killed the cat. Being inquisitive about other people's business, or what they think about us can lead us to make unfavorable decisions. If other people's antics towards us easily offend us, it's best to ignore them. If people bring up negativity, change the subject.

Actions speak louder than words. If our goal is to exercise goodness and maintain a level of integrity that is admirable, we cannot allow circumstances and people to determine how we behave. Remember, God is in control, so we shouldn't allow the actions of others to control our behaviors.

Temptations tested my morality. Just as I was reprimanded for accessing email accounts, I later realized a test was administered unto me. I could not worry about whether the enemy faced consequences for his/her actions or not. That should have not been my concern. When we delight ourselves in the Lord, we no longer focus on our enemies; we direct our attention to doing what is just.

I Sacrificed

I've made many sacrifices along the way. I've sacrificed my time for ministry. In all I've been through, I always made time to provide my son with more than what society determines as necessities. I teach my son about God, differences between right and wrong, being trustworthy, loving, and the value of hard work.

I've sacrificed my feelings, my time, my pride, my money and many more. I've sacrificed my body through abstinence, fasting, and dance. I worked hard to ensure I was getting stronger. It was not easy along the way and I should have lost my mind years ago. I learned that many people probably could not handle my journey. Nor can I handle someone else's. God was strengthening me this entire time for His glory because he loves me that much. I could have had an easy life with little hardships, but I would never improve if I always win. Do I like struggles or want trials? No. But, I know God loves beyond what we are used to seeing. After all, He sacrificed His son, Jesus for the remission of our sins. God showed me sacrificial love.

I Endured

I am still living through my journey. All of my goals have not been met, but my faith is stronger than ever. When times get tough, I reach for an edible fruit and I delve into the word and pray. I have my moments of desperation. I have my moments of anger. I have my moments of despair. I have my moments of disappointment. I have moments when I'm so confused! I'm human. However, I do my best to rely on individuals I can trust wholeheartedly and vent to them.

I also have my moments of success. I have celebratory moments. I have fun moments. I have breakthroughs. I have great memories. I am able to endure when I focus on the great things that occur rather than the oppositions. I am enduring.

I challenge you to Ex-E-R-C-I-S-E your core daily through the fruit of the spirit. Reflect on yourself and the people around you.

- Are you aware of how you interact with people?
- Are you cognizant of people in your personal space?
- Are you vulnerable to change for the better?
- Are you accepting of God's vision for your life?
- Is it your desire to become edified in the word of God?
- Are you seeking God daily?
- Are you honest with yourself?

I also challenge you to be more like Paul. Generate a list of people in your life who have blessed you and in return, pray God will bless them. Reflect on what they have done and be a blessing to someone else. A harmonious life is what God intended us to have. Let's keep the blessings flowing.

CONCLUSION

God is so amazing. As I admitted in this book, God challenged me from the time *The Core* was an idea, throughout the brainstorming process, and at each stage as I wrote. There were times when the enemy tried to distract and discourage me. There were moments when I was almost done, but distractions tried to hinder me from finishing. I continued to handle responsibilities, commitments, disappointments, weaknesses, and make adjustments on how I interact with people. As my sole purpose for writing this book was to pour wisdom onto others about Godly character, God placed me around people and in circumstances where I had to practice what I preached.

Obedience steered me from distractions. I was advised by friends to just write even when things were so disorganized in my life. I had to be vulnerable and pour out my heart on paper. Had I continued to organize thoughts in my mind, I can honestly say I would have never written a single page. That is how God allowed me to exercise my faith. Had I not moved when He told me to move, I would have never gotten closer to identifying what God's purpose is for me.

I had to use my own Ex-E-R-C-I-S-E model at each stage without even realizing it existed. God is using you as well. For those of you who are at a crossroad in your life and feel you are unable to make a decision or even have the energy to do anything, I encourage you to make a move. When Moses questioned his capabilities, God's presence gave him courage. When Job began to suffer tremendous loss, he still pushed through and maintained his faith. As a result, God blessed him with more than he had before. When Joseph experienced multiple hardships such as betrayal, slavery and imprisonment, he continued to work hard, kept his faith, and allowed God to lead him to rule a nation. Jesus said, "…'It is finished'…." (John 19:30, NIV), just before He gave up His spirit. When Jesus was betrayed by his own disciples, mocked and ridiculed by crowds, tortured, beaten, and belittled, He continued the race until the very end. He could have easily given up, but He understood His purpose and stayed on course until the very end.

As I mentioned in Chapter 2, in many cases, the flesh will wrestle against the spirit. Allow God to be your trainer. Exercise, and watch how strong your core become.

NOTES

(1907). Van Dyke, H. *Joyful, Joyful, We Adore Thee.* Retrieved from http://www.hymntime.com/tch/htm/j/o/y/f/joyful.htm

(2018). Transforming the understanding and treatment of mental illness. National Institute of Mental Health. Retrieved from https:// www. nimh.nih.gov/health/statistics/suicide.shtml#part_154973

(2019). Core. Cambridge English Dictionary. Retrieved June 11, 2018 from https://dictionary.cambridge.org/us/dictionary/english/core

**All scriptures were cited from https://www.biblegateway.com/ and https://www.biblestudytools.com/.

CPSIA information can be obtained
at www.ICGtesting.com
Printed in the USA
BVHW031133090819
555507BV00005B/44/P